Intimate Messages From Heaven

THE STORY OF
HOLY LOVE MINISTRIES

WAYNE WEIBLE
Internationally Acclaimed Author on
Apparitions of the Blessed Virgin Mary

Intimate Messages From Heaven

THE STORY OF
HOLY LOVE MINISTRIES

WAYNE WEIBLE

Intimate Messages from Heaven
The Story of Holy Love Ministries

First Printing: May 2016
Copyright: April 2016 by Wayne Weible

ISBN 978-0-9850548-9-2
Library of Congress Control Number: 2016907706

Printed by:
New Hope Press
Hiawassee, Georgia

www.newhopepresspub.com
Judith@newhopepresspub.com
Published in the United States of America

OTHER PUBLICATIONS BY WAYNE WEIBLE

Miracle at Medjugorje **Tabloid** (Weible Columns, Inc., 1986; 130
million copies)

Medjugorje: The Message (Paraclete Press 1989; (more than a
million copies sold)

Letters from Medjugorje (Paraclete Press 1991)

Medjugorje: The Mission (Paraclete Press 1993)

The Final Harvest (Paraclete Press 1999)

Final Harvest Revised (CMJ Marian Pub. 2003)

A Child Shall Lead Them (Paraclete Press 2005)

Medjugorje: The Message (Paraclete Press 2006) Hardcover
commemorative edition

The Medjugorje Prayer Book (Paraclete Press 2007)

Are The Medjugorje Apparitions Authentic? Co-authored with Dr.
Mark Miravalle (New Hope Press 2008)

The Medjugorje Fasting Book (New Hope Press 2010)

Medjugorje: The Last Apparition (New Hope Press 2013)

Medjugorje and the Eucharist (New Hope Press 2014)

DEDICATION

I dedicate this book to the people who shared their stories of conversion and healing through the good fruits of Holy Love Ministry. They stand as testament to the call of this mission to love God above all else and to love our neighbor as we love our self.

MESSAGES

A particular message reportedly received by visionary Maureen Sweeney-Kyle is posted at the end of each chapter. The selected messages range from those given in the early years to the present. Each message given in this format identifies whether it is from the Blessed Virgin Mary (by bold italic type) or God The Father and Jesus (by bold type) or a saint (regular type face). There is also a chapter where I focus on specific messages.

All Scriptural quotations are from **New American Bible, Revised Edition (NABRE)**.

ACKNOWLEDGMENTS

This book would not have been done without the request, encouragement and gentle urgings of the Most Blessed Virgin Mary through her words to Holy Love visionary Maureen Sweeney-Kyle. Thanks to Maureen and husband Don for their constant encouragement and total dedication to their calling.

Thanks to my wife Judith for her enduring patience and detailed editing, as well as putting up with my occasional procrastination. Judith is always there to encourage me and also have the tenacity to sincerely criticize when necessary.

Thanks to Joan Topazio at Holy Love for serving as liaison and critic. Also for her and husband Bob's contribution of their story on how they came to Holy Love.

I must include good friend Sandi Culley, who is always willing to assist me with her very astute acumen as to readability of my writings.

A book is never the lone work of the author. Without these wonderful people, I might still be laboring away on how to tell the story. I truly hope you enjoy it and learn from it.

INDEX

WHY WRITE ABOUT HOLY LOVE?

Questions are going to be asked of me: Why would you become involved and write about Holy Love Ministries when it is so controversial? What about the local Catholic Cleveland Diocese issuing an admonition, a warning to Catholics not to go there? Why risk damaging your journalistic integrity when your entire writing career has been focused on the apparitions of the Blessed Virgin Mary at Medjugorje?

Well, the answer to all such questions is easy enough for me to give. It is that I truly feel the Holy Love apparitions are authentic having been there numerous times and spent hours with the claimed visionary Maureen Sweeney-Kyle and her husband Don. That plus interviewing many pilgrims who have experienced miracles both spiritual and physical have been enough to convince me. Therefore, I accept the risk to my journalistic integrity with an open heart.

I feel that Heaven is once again gracing us—all of us—the great public of staunch believers, moderate believers, sometimes believers and even unbelievers, with another response to crisis. It is a "today" crisis within this continent north and south; and in Central America and South America. In fact, it is crisis all over the world.

So, let's take it a step further: I believe that the supernatural apparitions reportedly happening at Holy Love for the past 30 years are taking place in answer to the crisis. It is occurring in conjunction with other known and unknown claimed apparitions throughout the world, mainly by the Blessed Virgin. I believe it is as authentic as Medjugorje, which I consider to be the main hub of Marian apparitions occurring now. Other noted places of past apparitions are Garabandal, Spain; Betania, Venezuela; and of course, Kibeho in Rwanda, Africa. There are others of less renown—that is, people experiencing inner locutions and visionaries confined to countries, regions, communities and even prayer groups.

Throughout the history of Marian apparitions the Mother of Jesus Christ is sent to earth by God to literally shore up the faith of the children of God. She does so through chosen souls whom we identify as visionaries or receivers of inner locutions. She is sent to meet crisis head-on. So powerful is the crisis not only in our beloved country of the United States of America but virtually *everywhere* in the world, that God the Father chooses to allow Himself, Jesus, Saint Joseph and a variety of other saints to join the Blessed Mother at Holy Love in bringing messages of renewal and much-needed hope.

Holy Love Ministries began when the Blessed Virgin Mary suddenly appeared to Maureen Sweeney-Kyle during Adoration of the Blessed Sacrament in a small church in the suburbs of Cleveland,

Ohio. From that startling experience, the Ministry grew by small, difficult steps to where it is today, a far-reaching ecumenical ministry based on simple prayer, meditation and living a life of personal holiness through Holy Love.

You will find here the history of the Ministry. You will also discover improbable stories of spiritual conversion. Most surprising is that you will learn of the tremendous endorsements by highly recognized theologians, all of which, ironically, are priests in the Catholic Church.

The most important element you will discover is the humility and directness of the messages given to Maureen. My hope is that they will touch you as deeply as they have touched so many millions of people, including me. That is reason enough for me to have written this book and to possibly risk my reputation as a journalist.

God bless you.

—Wayne Weible

ONE

———

DISCERNMENT

There are missions, sects and cults *ad infinitum* based on spiritual faith or belief of one kind or another scattered throughout the world. There are also endless numbers of people claiming they receive direct messages or visions from God in the form of Jesus, the Holy Spirit or the Blessed Virgin Mary. Such claims are classified as *private* revelations as opposed to *public* revelations, the latter being Holy Scriptures of the new and old Testaments.

The quintessential question to be asked concerning these matters is this: How do you know that a group or individual with such a claim might possibly be authentic? How do you separate the authentic from the phony; or scam artists; or, those with over-active imaginations— or those challenged by mental instability?

Many such groups or individuals claiming to have singular or ongoing supernatural experiences are sincere in their belief and in trying to bring people into a closer relationship with God. However, others are just as motivated—although not by faith but often by the lure of quick riches and/or that elusive fifteen minutes of fame.

Thus, the difficulty in judgment of these events is in knowing how to tell the good from the bad—the sheep from the goats. Cutting to the heart of the matter, there are three general methods of fairly gauging the authenticity of such groups or individuals on an unofficial basis. The three methods listed here are but three of many. Still, they may be enough to give reason for a church or related organization to investigate such a claim—or, for an individual to believe.

Here are the ways to broadly discern if a claimed supernatural event may possibly be authentic: first, in the face of such controversy and doubt, what kind of spiritual fruit has it produced over an extended period of time? The key here is the "extended" period of time, that is, for example a period of several years or more. Is the fruit good? Does it result in consistent spiritual conversions?

Second, are the messages given to the claimed visionary or visionaries in line with Holy Scripture? That is easy enough to verify as any good theologian can quickly detect if such messages contain heresy or blasphemy. It only takes a tiny dose of such poisons to expose a hidden agenda of false teachings.

Third, is the recipient of the grace sincerely humble and living a life aligned with Holy Scripture? That would include regular attendance at church services, actively attempting to assist those in need and generally living a consistent devout life.

These three measuring rods of any alleged apparition, locution or similar supernatural event normally in a general fashion separate the good and the true from the false and the bad.

Holy Love Ministries is a case in point. It can positively pass all three of the listed measuring rods in the affirmative. The ministry began in early 1985 with the claim of an extremely shy, devout, Catholic woman named Maureen Sweeney-Kyle. In January 1985 while at Adoration of the Blessed Sacrament in a small church, Maureen claims that the Blessed Virgin Mary suddenly appeared to her. The apparition was swift in coming and quickly gone before Maureen could fully grasp its reality.

Within a matter of days, the apparitions and then messages continued from that day on, which Maureen soon shared with a small, supportive prayer group.

From the support of this tiny group who believed Maureen's claim, Holy Love Ministries has its roots even though it would not be formally known as Holy Love for more than a decade. The little mustard seed of its startling beginning has grown into a massive bush of incredible spiritual conversions that have included spiritual and physical healings, giving further credence to its authenticity.

Today, Holy Love Ministries incorporates a huge international following with thousands in attendance at special feast day celebrations. Many come regularly to the evening service for the praying of the holy rosary. The grounds and facilities contain a series of practical buildings, a large gathering area and several small lakes and spiritually themed smaller buildings scattered on a huge parcel of land in the suburbs of Cleveland, Ohio. From the beginning it has produced good, solid spiritual fruits over the 30 years of existence undergoing several changes in name over that timeframe.

Adding authenticity to its general goal of bringing people into a personal relationship with God mainly through prayer, meditation and living Holy Love, there is nothing in any of the alleged messages from Heaven given to visionary Maureen that has been found to be out of line with Holy Scripture—or the doctrines of the Roman Catholic Church, of which Maureen and her husband are members and daily communicants.

Despite these good traits, almost from its beginning days Holy Love has been steeped in controversy. Most of it stems from an initial lack of interest to eventual rejection by the Catholic Diocese of Cleveland, Ohio, which, contrary to what they have published and publically stated has yet to conduct any kind of an in depth, objective formal investigation of Maureen's claims or the messages she has received. Meanwhile, the tiny supportive prayer group that began developing around the claims of Maureen has grown into an incredible daily ministry that has produced enormously good fruits. Thousands of people throughout the continent of North America, from Canada to Mexico, have found spiritual conversion through pilgrimage to its site. The same is true with pilgrims coming from Central America and South America.

Regardless of such good fruits, the controversy over its authenticity continues—contrasted by the conversions and spiritual miracles that are ongoing at the site.

The same set of circumstances at Holy Love applies to another famous, ongoing claimed Marian apparition site in the village of

Medjugorje. Six teenage Croatians claimed that they have been receiving visions and messages from the Blessed Virgin Mary since June
24, 1981, which reportedly continue daily since. It has grown into the
most popular apparition site in the Catholic Church with pilgrims
coming there from all over the world.

Ironically, I found my spiritual conversion through Medjugorje, located deep in the mountains of Bosnia-Hercegovina. Five years
after its beginning when I first learned of it, the messages and good
fruits of this incredible supernatural event so deeply touched me
that I sold my successful businesses in order to devote all my time to
spreading its messages of prayer, fasting and penance. It has allegedly
been ongoing daily for more than 34 years as of this writing. I firmly
believe it to be authentic.

As with Holy Love Ministries, Medjugorje has produced a long
history of outstandingly good spiritual fruits. The two sites share a
common problem; both have been under siege from a source neither
would have thought to be so opposed: The local hierarchy of the Roman Catholic Church. For Holy Love Ministries, it is the Diocese
of Cleveland, Ohio; for Medjugorje, it has been and still is the local
bishop of the Mostar Diocese, which includes the parish of the little
village.

During the long history of the Medjugorje apparitions, two serving bishops of the diocese during its claimed beginning and subsequent years have stated their personal disbelief in the apparitions and
have bitterly opposed those who do. Both bishops, the current one
Bishop Ratko Peric, and his predecessor the late Bishop Paolo Zanic,
vigorously sought to bring them to an end, claiming they are a cruel

hoax created by the local Franciscan priests in charge of the parish to make huge sums of money.

Bishop Zanic, who in the beginning firmly believed in the claimed apparitions at Medjugorje but later inexplicably changed his opinion, formed two separate local investigative commissions in the early years of the apparitions with both coming to a negative conclusion on their authenticity. Both investigations, purposely loaded by the bishop with handpicked members who did not believe in the apparitions, would unprecedentedly have the findings rejected by the Vatican for obvious bias. Such continued acts led the Vatican to remove the local bishop's authority over the apparitions and to take direct charge, again an unprecedented act by the Holy See.

As of this writing, the Church has stated that the apparitions at Medjugorje cannot be affirmed as authentic, nor can they be confirmed as not authentic. Therefore, they remain in a neutral state and under investigation. This declaration was formally established in the fall of 1991 by a commission of former bishops of Yugoslavia and is known as the Zadar Declaration. It is the official position of the Catholic Church as the apparitions continue daily.

Essentially, the same set of circumstances as applied at Medjugorje is true of the claimed messages given at Holy Love, even though as an ecumenical ministry, that is, open to all people of all faiths, *they do not fall under the rule of the local Catholic bishop!* Yet, the bishop continues to discourage people of his diocese as well as those from other states and countries from going to Holy Love on pilgrimage. It leaves one wondering why a Catholic bishop would actively discourage souls from going to a place of prayer with an incredible track record of great spiritual fruits, including hundreds of physical and spiritual healings.

The one sure way, as stated earlier, is to test the fruits of a claimed apparition through Holy Scripture. An important question concerning such allegations that should be asked is this: Are the reported messages, events or circumstances surrounding a claim of an apparition or locution in line with the teaching of the Gospels? Let's take a look.

As Holy Scripture tells us: **Thus, you will know them by their fruits** (Matt. 7:20). This singular line of Scripture should be enough impetus to cause doubters of such groups or individuals to dig a little deeper in seeking its authenticity. Alas, with the human race, more is often required. How many people take the time necessary to look at the fruits of such spiritual missions or individuals over a period of time long enough to make a proper discernment? How many are already opposed and with noticeable stubbornness refuse out of spiritual pride to change even when given solid evidence?

I am reminded of a time in the early nineties when I was invited to attend a special Saturday morning prayer group inspired by the apparitions of the Blessed Virgin at Medjugorje. It was an extra special occasion in that one of the visionaries from Medjugorje would be there along with one of the Franciscan priests from the parish. Marija Pavlovic was the visionary and the Franciscan was Father Slavko Barbaric, who had become the main spiritual advisor to the visionaries. He was well-known among the followers of the apparitions because of his endless work in the village to bring order to the event and assure that a proper spiritual process be established in spreading the powerful messages the Virgin was giving to the village and the world. Additionally, Father Slavko was well educated, holding two PhD degrees.

As everyone settled in, Fr. Slavko began his talk. Near the end, he opened the session to questions; immediately, a woman raised her hand and asked: "Father Slavko, what are we to think of so many claimed apparitions and locutions of the Blessed Virgin Mary occurring throughout the country and the world?"

After a few moments of reflection, Father Slavko quietly answered: "You should believe in them until you are sure they are not from God."

Everyone sat in silence contemplating the straightforward, simple yet profound answer. Fr. Slavko then expounded on his answer explaining that to judge such an alleged supernatural event either way may be going up against the Holy Spirit, which of course, is the only way any supernatural grace is given to the world. It made sense.

Holy Scripture gives us yet another formula, which fully backs up what Fr. Slavko had stated in his answer. In Acts 5:33-39, it states: **When they heard this, they were enraged and wanted to kill them. But a Pharisee in the council named Gamaliel, a teacher of the law, respected by all the people, stood up and ordered the men to be put outside for a short time. Then he said to them, "Fellow Israelites consider carefully what you propose to do to these men. For some time ago Theudas rose up, claiming to be somebody, and a number of men, about four hundred, joined him; but he was killed, and all who followed him were dispersed and disappeared. After him Judas the Galilean rose up at the time of the census and got people to fol-**

low him; he also perished, and all who followed him were scattered. So in the present case, I tell you, keep away from these men and let them alone; because if this plan or this undertaking is of human origin, it will fail; but if it is of God, you will not be able to overthrow them — in that case you may even be found fighting against God!"

To believe in the grace of the alleged apparitions of the Blessed Virgin Mary at the village of Medjugorje, or those given to Maureen at Holy Love Ministries, requires the *proper spiritual discernment.* The Holy Spirit gift of Discernment comes with full acceptance of the reality of God and of course through His Word as we see from the above readings. However, it is only the beginning.

The gift of discernment usually leads one to further explore. That is what I learned through the apparitions at Medjugorje and then later through Holy Love. However, the way it personally happened at Holy Love left no doubt in my heart as you will see in the next chapter.

∽

Message given by the Blessed Virgin Mary on March 21, 1993:

I am Mary, Queen of Heaven and Earth--Queen of the Most Holy Rosary. All praise be to Jesus. (I answered, "Now and forever.") *My little child, the hour of great decision has come when those who seek to remain faithful to My Heart will need to prudently choose. Satan will divide My Son's Church upon earth. He will come clothed in reason and goodness. And you must be careful to remain faithful to Church Tradition as it stands now under John Paul II. The ensuing confusion will bring bishop against bishop, parent against child, husband against wife. Some Masses will not be valid under Church law, and many will be deceived. You will need to be strong. Persevere in Tradition as I have taught you. My mantle is over you. My Immaculate Heart is the Refuge of all who are faithful to Church Tradition. Therefore, be at peace.*

TWO

I BELIEVE

In the time of active involvement with the people who established and operate Holy Love Ministries, I have seen nothing but good, sound spiritual fruits that continue to convert and nourish the tens of thousands of individuals who come there.

Ironically, I had met Maureen Sweeney-Kyle and first heard of Holy Love when she came to one of my talks on Medjugorje in the Cleveland area somewhere in the late eighties. Our meeting was brief, just long enough for her to timidly tell me that she was receiving messages from the Blessed Mother.

Surprisingly, I believed this timid woman but as with so many claims that I had heard in the few years of involvement with Medjugorje, I simply filed it away in my mind. Yet, from that time, I began to pray daily for Maureen, adding her name to the list of visionaries of Medjugorje and a few others I met along the way and felt were authentic. The list is short with the primary concentration on Medjugorje with other claims in the memory bank.

My involvement in the apparitions of Medjugorje came about in an extremely unique way in that I felt the Blessed Virgin literally asking me to give up my life in the world of secularism and business in order to write about and spread her messages being given to the visionaries. It was as if the entire words from her were placed in my heart at one time. Most importantly, there was no doubt in my mind that this shocking event was real.

I was a lukewarm Protestant at the time this message was placed in my heart. I had never given two thoughts to the Blessed Virgin Mary. In fact, I really did not fully believe in God even though I was active in my Lutheran church. It was such a powerful and real experience that as it actually came to pass and I began writing about it, which brought requests for speaking engagements, I paid little or no attention to other claims of apparitions--including those of Holy Love Ministries.

Years later I began receiving calls from Maureen's husband, Don Kyle, inviting me to come to Holy Love to give a talk. I politely declined using excuses such as being too busy with Medjugorje. Undeterred, Don would call again every three months or so, until one time, I simply did not have an excuse not to accept his invitation. Reluctantly, I agreed to come to the site for a December celebration of another famous apparition of the Blessed Virgin Mary at Guadalupe in Mexico City, Mexico.

I arrived in Cleveland in bitter cold weather, offset by the warmth and cordial greeting from Don Kyle as he met me at the airport. Within minutes, I felt very comfortable with him; still, I was not ready to fully embrace the reality of Holy Love. However, Don's gentle voice and casual manner soon had me feeling very welcome and I decided to keep an open mind.

We arrived at the modest home of Don and Maureen on the grounds of Holy Love, which also included three attached apartments normally reserved for priests or other special guests. I would be staying in the one closest to their quarters. Don suggested that I rest for a while and then we would go over the schedule for the day and that evening. As I arranged my belongings and was in the process of removing a sweater I was wearing, I murmured out loud in a low voice, "I wonder if this place is real—"

Before I could finish the thought, I literally felt the Blessed Virgin place a message in my heart that simply said, *You're here!*

I stopped for several seconds with the sweater half off, somewhat stunned by the blunt confirmation. The Blessed Virgin's words to me were as clear as if I had heard someone verbally speaking to me. As I finished removing the sweater, I smiled and thought: "Okay, that's pretty strong!"

I sat on the edge of the bed contemplating her words and realized that there was indeed a purpose in my praying for this shy woman Maureen all these years. Holy Love Ministries was not much different than the apparitions at Medjugorje. I felt Our Lady by the power of the Holy Spirit was definitely here.

An hour later I met with Don and Maureen. They explained to me that the crowds usually came during the special feast days, with smaller groups and individuals coming almost daily. Every evening the rosary was prayed in a large inside assembly hall for the visiting pilgrims and volunteer members of the staff. Holy Love had grown over the years to the point that larger facilities were needed. They had been at this site since 1996 and had started using the title of Holy Love Ministries at that time.

Maureen explained to me that the Blessed Mother would usually come almost daily while Jesus came frequently. They would dictate word by word the messages and Maureen would write them on index cards. During public appearances Maureen would repeat them word-by-word in a low whisper for Don who would then record them on a small tape recorder. He would then write down the message. Throughout the formation years there were thousands of messages given predominantly by the Blessed Virgin and Jesus and on a random basis, also by saints and angels. Every message was recorded and placed in storage.

Late that evening, we proceeded to a small canvas-covered building located in a large field called the United Hearts Field, where Maureen and Don as well as several guests, including me, would be seated for the praying of the rosary and the eventual apparition. Other guests were usually visiting priests. I was totally unprepared for the event wearing thin-soled shoes and a light sport coat. Don soon gave me a heavy jacket saying, "You might need this as we will be here for awhile."

We were in an open field covered in snow and it was cold—really cold! I was surprised to discover that the Blessed Virgin would not give the message until midnight and up to that time we would be praying the rosary. Even more surprising was the crowd of nearly

3,000 people huddled together awaiting the words from Heaven to be given to Maureen. It was, in a word, awesome.

Soon I forgot where we were and that it was cold. Like the crowd, I was immersed in the prayer of the rosary, which seemed to suspend all feelings of discomfort from the cold and a lack of sleep.

I returned to my room a few hours later, back to reality, with frozen feet and a pair of shoes I was sure were ruined from the slush. More importantly, there was no longer any doubt or reservation concerning the authenticity of the apparitions given to Maureen Sweeney-Kyle at Holy Love Ministries.

I returned to my home a day later from Holy Love as a true believer—so much so that I decided it was worth considering writing about it and letting the world know.

∽

Message from the Blessed Virgin to Maureen on May 1, 1993:

I want to teach you to be disciples of the grace of My Heart. Dear children, realize that all things are a grace and dependent upon grace. See how little you are compared to this magnificent gift. When you come to realize your littleness, I will build you up in grace to accomplish God's Will through you. I will nurture your little hearts in My motherly grace so that you will be all God wants you to be, and then you will answer My call to you.

THREE

THE MESSENGER

Who is this person at Holy Love Ministries who claims to receive messages from Heaven? Is she believable? What proof is there to verify her claims?

These are valid questions to be asked of someone who states that she believes she is receiving personal messages from heavenly beings.

The person, Maureen Sweeney-Kyle, is the alleged visionary of Holy Love Ministries. She is a shy, quiet woman who is a life-long resident of the Cleveland, Ohio community. She is most definitely believable in my opinion because of her sincerity, transparency and overwhelming humility noticeable in her every action. As for the "proof" of her claims, more than 30 years of apparitions with tens of thousands of messages has left a pattern of extremely good spiritual fruits, just as outlined in the first chapter of this book, as a general measuring rod. Add to this literally thousands of physical and spiritual healings that have occurred at the site, many of which have been medically and scientifically verified.

Maureen was the younger of two sisters born to parents divided in faith; her father was Catholic who always practiced his faith from an Irish American home. Her mother was Protestant and a bit more into living a faith-filled life. She later converted to the Catholic faith and had a good influence on her younger daughter.

The often sickly and frail Maureen was drawn to the prayer of the rosary at an early age and developed a strong love for the Blessed Virgin, possibly giving reason for her later being chosen for such an awesome grace. She stated in an interview in early 2015 that she could not remember a time when there wasn't a little statue of the Mother of Jesus in her room starting from about the age of seven. After her first Holy Communion, she received a rosary and later was given a book about the apparitions at Fatima, Portugal. Thus from childhood, Maureen developed a love for the Virgin never imagining that somewhere in the future she would be chosen for such a holy task.

Maureen led a fairly normal life as a child. She attended public schools in the area and went on to earn a college degree. She worked at various jobs and was married at the age of 24.

Maureen continued on her spiritual journey, attending daily Mass often and always praying the holy rosary. One day in early January 1985 as she participated in Adoration of the Blessed Sacrament at a nearby Catholic church, she was startled to unexpectedly see the Blessed Virgin Mary suddenly appear on the right side of the tabernacle, standing just a small distance behind it. She was dressed in a light pink and smoky lavender-colored dress, holding a large beaded rosary in her hands. Maureen sat there, dazed and wondered, "Am I the only one seeing her?"

People got up from their seats and moved around while others left and some were just coming in. It struck Maureen that no one else was seeing what she was seeing. She later described the moment adding, "All of a sudden, the fifty Hail Mary beads of the large rosary she was holding turned into the shapes of the fifty states (of the United States). Then as quickly as she had appeared, she left. I didn't know why she was there, but I thought maybe she wants me to pray for the country."

Life for Maureen drastically changed from that miraculous moment of seeing the Blessed Virgin Mary. Yes, she had maintained an intimate love for the Virgin but now to actually see her in supernatural apparition? She immediately found the man who ran the Adoration service and told him what she had just experienced in seeing the Blessed Virgin. She then pleaded with him to please not let others know about it as they might think of her as someone looking for attention or maybe even think that she was crazy.

Shortly after the initial contact, Maureen began receiving more frequent messages, first from Jesus and then more from the Virgin. Still she did not tell anyone other than the man who had run the Adoration. She then joined a charismatic prayer group hoping this would be what Jesus and Mary wanted. One evening she was shocked when a man from the group got to his feet and said: "There's someone here who is getting heavenly messages and not speaking out or revealing them."

Maureen thought: "Oh no!" The man suggested that they turn off the air conditioner in case the unidentified person had a quiet voice. She immediately knew that everyone would know she was the person he was talking about. She ran out of the building in tears and never returned to that prayer group.

In a later interview in 2006, Maureen said, "I finally decided to go back to the man who had run the Adoration the night Our Lady first appeared. He suggested that I give him the messages and he would then read them. No one would have to know it was me who was receiving the messages. I agreed and from that time on I started to write down the messages."

Sadly, as the apparitions not only continued, but became more frequent, Maureen's marriage began to erode; her husband, a devout Catholic, just could not grasp the sudden change of course created by the apparitions. He did not feel comfortable that his wife and mother of their four children was suddenly a visionary, nor could he cope with such a dramatic change of life. They were divorced in 1997.

It was an extremely traumatic time for Maureen. She could not comprehend how she could be receiving supernatural apparitions from Jesus and the Blessed Virgin Mary that they would eventually contribute to bringing an end to her marriage. She knew in her heart that the apparitions were really happening to her and she prayed for things to work out with her and her husband. Unfortunately, they did not. She filed for annulment and was granted it a year later.

Happiness would finally come years later when Maureen met Don Kyle, a former police sergeant in the Cleveland area, who at the time was living in Florida. Maureen had come to the Florida area to give her witness on her experiences with the apparitions. Don was immediately impressed by the visionary and fully believed her story. Six years before, he had taken early retirement from police work and moved to Florida.

It was in the fall of 1989 that Don picked up the first publication I had written about the apparitions at Medjugorje and how it had affected me. He had been a daily communicant since 1987. Something clicked within him that caused him to believe this was authentic.

Approximately two months after meeting Maureen, Don returned to Cleveland. He immediately sought a prayer group in the area, which led him to Maureen's little assembly of believers. He saw Maureen as someone very special and treated her with the greatest respect. After several years of low-key courtship, Don and Maureen would marry in 1997, with Don eventually assuming a leadership role in the ministry.

Maureen describes some details of the Virgin's visits to her: "Our Lady always appears in a very bright light, quite often floating on a cloud. Many times she has angels with her. She brings a heavenly presence with her. Our Lady's face is oval-shaped and her skin is a milky white. She has brown eyes and her hair is medium brown, always parted in the middle and reaches just below her shoulders. Usually, most of it is concealed under her veil. Her voice is melodic and velvety. I've never heard a voice like it on earth. As breathtaking as her physical appearance is, her real beauty comes from within. It is this inner beauty that makes you feel a sense of peace, even when she speaks about unpleasant things. Sometimes she cries and I would do anything to make her happy again. She comes to reconcile mankind to God through Holy Love."

Here again is substantiation that Maureen is at the least seeing something extraordinary. Her description of the Blessed Virgin Mary is extremely similar to other descriptions by other claimed visionaries. Sometimes the color of the eyes and hair may vary (Actually, it seems that the Blessed Virgin Mary usually appears as a member of the culture or country where she is appearing. For instance in Medjugorje, she looks very Croatian; to Maureen, she appears as an American).

The reluctant visionary remained anonymous for the first nine years of the apparitions, which suited her fine. Then, the Blessed Mother asked her to step out in faith and to begin to speak publicly on the messages. Of course that would mean that everyone would then know she was the "anonymous" visionary, and that it would take great fortitude for her to do this.

For the next several years, Maureen traveled throughout the country and also several foreign countries. However, Maureen eventually had to end the public speaking engagements due to health concerns. It was also a personal blessing and relief in that she did not enjoy appearing or speaking to the public. She did manage to make pilgrimage to the Medjugorje apparition site three times in the late eighties. Of course, she never told the local visionaries about her experiences; nor did she consider her grace in the same light as the apparitions at Medjugorje. She knew little about Medjugorje until after her gift of grace began in the adoration chapel.

Maureen and Don were graced by an audience with Pope John Paul II In August 1999, that had been arranged by an archbishop from Africa who had been to Holy Love, recognized it for its tremendously good fruits and was happy to do this for them. Maureen presented books and documents about Holy Love. It was definitely a highlight of her life.

Over the years, the ministry of Holy Love developed and evolved into what it is today. Word began to spread about Maureen's supernatural gift and simultaneously, she started to take on more duties, such as meeting with Catholic priests and nuns, and occasionally other clergy from Protestant faiths for counseling at their request—in spite of her shyness. This, to her, is still an important part of the ministry.

The shy visionary will not sit for recorded interviews with secular media or individuals or have her picture taken for public use. In essence, she wants no attention beyond the fact that she receives these graces from Heaven. As of this writing, more than 30,000 messages have been given to Maureen. An interesting thing I have observed is that Maureen will give the message as it has been given to her and later will ask someone about what a certain word contained in the message means. She is at a loss to explain how she can use the word in the message without knowing what it means. Maureen is by no means lacking in intelligence as she graduated from four years of college; but as she readily admits, she has a limited vocabulary.

Maureen Sweeney-Kyle is as she puts it, is the "least likely person" one would suspect to be given such a grace as a visionary. But that is exactly the reason why she was chosen and why the messages she receives could have only come from a higher source. Maureen still suffers from a variety of health issues, keeping her in a chronic frail state of health.

True to her statement of not being "important", Maureen wishes to keep this somewhat personal glimpse of her to a minimum. Thus, I shall comply.

We will see more of the character of the Holy Love visionary in the following chapters as we continue to tell the story.

∾

Message to Maureen from Our Lady, October 24, 1993:

Our Lady came in gray with a red lining in Her mantle. She spreads Her hands and says:

All praise be to Jesus. I am the Mother of Jesus crucified. My angel, my little child, I invite you to further understand in your heart that Holy Love is a selfless love. It opposes the world and self. In like manner, holy perfection is a selfless perfection in that the soul chooses to perfect himself in holiness to please God. My daughter, as I, your Mother, stood beneath the Cross, I suffered everything for love of God and for souls. I suffered this way in Holy Love and it was holy suffering. Holy suffering has no regard for self, but sees only what is being accomplished for souls. The more the soul is steeped in Holy Love, the more holy his suffering. So then, even at the darkest moment, the soul sees God's purpose and unites himself to God. I am showing you all of this in the Light of Truth so that as error spreads, as it will, you can be light to others. Pray for the love of souls.

FOUR

THE STORY

The beginning of Holy Love Ministries was, of course, the startling moment when visionary Maureen Kyle saw and heard the Blessed Virgin Mary during adoration at a small Catholic church. From its initial contact the ministry began its progress to where and what it is today.

The first thought of Maureen, a devout Catholic, was to find a priest and tell him what had occurred during adoration when the Virgin first spoke to her. She really did not know where it would go from there, still in shock that it had happened at all. The original priest whom she told what had happened believed her. He listened and attempted to assist Maureen. After some time, Maureen was directed by the Blessed Mother to go to a different spiritual director.

The Blessed Virgin then told her in March 1987 that she was now coming to her under the title of, "Our Lady, Protectress of the Faith" and to go to the bishop's office to affirm the use of that title along with a simple prayer. She was dismayed when informed by a member of the diocesan staff (not the bishop) that such a title was not necessary because Our Lady already had "too many titles." Also, it was told to her that the Holy Spirit is known as the Protector of the Faith.

As if to confirm the new title, four months later the Blessed Virgin reportedly began appearing to a young woman in Ecuador, South America named Patricia Talbot in August 1988 asking for just about the same criteria that was asked of Maureen. Shortly thereafter, the local ordinary approved the use of the title and association under the name: "Guardian of the Faith," literally the same title given to Maureen.

It was all down hill with the Catholic Diocese of Cleveland from that time until today. Maureen, who went to the bishop's office out of obedience to the Blessed Virgin, was written off as "just another person whose imagination had run way with her." However, the title of Our Lady, Protectress of the Faith, served the fledgling ministry from 1986 to 1990.

It was a difficult beginning for Holy Love Ministries due mainly to the vague statements and innuendos of the diocese. Over the years it became evident that if it were to succeed as a place of spiritual growth and mission, it would have to be done by the work of Don and Maureen, a handful of close friends and believers and a large assembly of volunteers. Without such support, the Ministry in all likelihood would have failed.

However, according to Maureen, the Blessed Mother and Jesus were always there to guide them and to encourage them. In 1994, it was the Blessed Virgin who asked that the Ministry become ecumenical so that it could reach all people of all faiths. As always, the Ministry complied.

Progress was slow and at times painful due to a constant lack of funds. Yet, when things seemed hopeless, the Ministry would suddenly be rescued by a few anonymous monetary donations that helped fill the needs to permanently establish the necessary programs. There was never an organized plan in the early years to seek donations from the pilgrims who came there, nor was there any formulated effort to continually seek donations by mail or electronic means. Regardless, there always seem to be just enough funds to carry on.

From 1990 through 1993, the ministry was known as Project Mercy, which entailed the establishment of a nationwide anti-abortion Rosary Crusade. From this program a new rosary was formed that consisted of the Hail Mary beads containing a small figure of an unborn child. Literally tens of thousands of these rosaries have been distributed throughout the states, Canada, Mexico, Central America and South America. They continue to be part of this incredible effort to bring the horror of abortion of the unborn to an end.

Finally in March 1994, a new title was given to the ministry: Holy Love Ministries, formed again through the wishes of the Blessed Mother and Jesus. It would now have the goal of propagation of the teachings of Holy and Divine Love to all the children of God. The basic tenant is the very words given by Jesus in Scripture. We quote from the Gospel of Matthew: **"You shall love the Lord your God with all your heart, and with all your soul, and with all your mind"** (Matthew 22: 37). The second is: **"You shall love your neighbor as yourself"** (Matthew 22:39).

Later, Maureen was instructed by Our Lady to dig for a well in the back of the small property that they were presently using. She found a spring on May 5 and from its water, healings began immediately. The spring was to be called "Maranatha" which means, "Come, Lord Jesus." (More on the Spring in Chapter Ten). Word quickly spread about the healings and the conversions occurring at this place called Holy Love.

The next month, June, a massive crowd of more than 2,000 gathered at the site, prompting the local police to gain a court order closing the site citing the reason being the crowds too large with no control and causing unsafe conditions. The order caused the Ministry to vacate that location within six months. It was soon evident that a larger piece of property would be needed.

Efforts to spread the messages slowly began to take on a new form with a surprisingly strong word-of-mouth informally assisting the progress. The prominent need was a permanent site to establish a home for the ministry; thus, Don began a search for a suitable piece of property. Finally in 1995, the right property was found. Holy Love Ministries soon had a permanent home on 82 acres of property located in Lorain County, Ohio.

Shortly after settling on the new location, the Blessed Virgin once again directed Maureen where to dig to establish a new Maranatha Spring of healing waters. And, as with the first Maranatha Spring, miraculous healings and conversions began occurring immediately. It continues as of this writing. There are hundreds of testimonies citing the healing powers of this implausible Maranatha Spring. It brings many people of all faiths to Holy Love based on word of mouth accounts by those who have experienced the effects of the holy water.

Now with a new permanent location and with room for growth, huge crowds coming for the special feast days would gather in a large open field called the United Hearts Field. They did so regardless of the weather. Late in the evening, usually around 11:30 P.M., the praying of the rosary would commence, starting with the Glorious Mysteries, interchanging between English and Spanish—as there is normally a significant contingent of Hispanics present. Somewhere along the way as this occurs, Maureen suddenly informs her husband Don that "Our Lady is here." He then announces it to those leading the rosary; they in turn tell the crowd: "Please kneel!"

At that time everyone kneels while Maureen receives the apparition message. In a hushed whisper she repeats slowly the words of the message to Don who then records it as it is given. Afterwards, the rosary continues as Don quietly writes the message down from the recording. It is then later read to the crowd after the completion of the rosary prayers.

The majority of the messages given to Maureen come from Jesus Christ and the Blessed Virgin Mary. Other messages are also received from several saints and angels. All of the spiritual messages, regardless of the giver, lend solid support to the two great commandments given to the world through Holy Scripture by Jesus. The overriding objective of the ministry is to bring about complete world peace through sincere prayer, an end to abortion and the spiritual conversion of as many hearts as possible. That includes all peoples of all faiths who sincerely seek God.

As an ecumenical organization, the spiritual messages of Holy Love promotes Christian unity—as Jesus prayed in John 17:20-21: **"I ask not only on behalf of these, but also on behalf of those who will believe in me through their word, that they may all be one. As you, Father, are in me and I am in you, may they also be in us, so that the world may believe that you have sent me."**

Opponents of Holy Love see the decision to be ecumenical as avoiding control from the Catholic Diocese of Cleveland. They quickly point out that so much of its program of prayer and embracement of saints and angels is widely considered to be Catholic in nature. Yet the Church itself gives ecumenism the proper credibility. The Catechism of the Catholic Church, Section 821, describes ecumenism as "Prayer in common, because change of heart and holiness of life, along with public and private prayer for the unity of Christendom, should be regarded as the soul of the whole ecumenical movement, and merits the name 'spiritual ecumenism'."

Thus, the praying of the rosary as well as other Catholic prayers and symbols are primary parts of the ministry. To exclude them from the Ministry would be to say Catholics must not be part of the ecumenical movement. This would be contrary to the local Bishop's and the Holy Father's ecumenical efforts. People do come from all faiths, even though the predominant majority of pilgrims are Catholic. The people who come there know this. There is no attempt to lure them to the site by pretending to be fully Catholic. They know before they come. The common denominator is encouragement of respect for people of all faiths. That isn't to say all faiths are equal but that we as

Christians are called to love and respect people of all faiths. It is up to God to decide beyond that.

Holy Love Ministries is also strongly guided by Catholic Canon law 215, which states: "The Christian faithful are at liberty freely to found and direct associations for purposes of charity or piety or for the promotion of the Christian vocation in the world and to hold meetings for the common pursuit of these purposes. The association, which a believer founds, can remain a de facto association *without official juridic. Therefore, the Ministry as an ecumenical body is not affiliated with a particular diocese* (emphasis in italics added).

Such adherence to Catholic canon law comes from the fact that Maureen and Don *are* Catholics and always attend Holy Mass regularly, as do many of the volunteers at Holy Love. Catholic pilgrims who come to the site are encouraged to also attend Mass and the Ministry makes available a list of sites of nearby Catholic churches. All people from all faiths are welcome to come and pray for unity in the "Body of Christ" (Ephesians 4:4-6) at Holy Love.

As further clarification and confirmation, and a direct answer to the diocese's charge that Holy Love is out to "get rich" on donations from the visiting pilgrims, Catholic Canon law 216 states that a believer has the right to promote a ministry that obviously includes voluntary fund raising. Financial contributions to the Ministry are encouraged but are not demanded nor pushed beyond the ordinary. In fact, in the history of the ministry only one time (in 1994) have they sent a letter to supporters asking for financial aid and support of their efforts to spread the messages of spiritual conversion through Holy Love. There are no organized campaigns to raise donations—as is the case with most faith-based organizations and churches. At the same time, Holy Love Ministries always encourages people to support their local parishes or churches.

To put it bluntly, Holy Love Ministry is a place of prayer and meditation. It survives on the voluntary donations from the pilgrims and benefactors, and the sales of books and related goods. The property now contains modest buildings for meetings and organized public prayer. There are several small lakes and sites for specific intentions. Several times each year there are special celebrations of feast days attended by large crowds, who gather in an open field for prayer and the apparition to be given to Maureen at that time. These meetings usually occur late at night with the apparition coming near midnight. The celebrations take place regardless of the weather conditions within reasonable boundaries.

Beyond these special outdoor celebrations, there are *no public religious services of any denomination* held on the public grounds in Elyria.

Thousands of people follow the daily messages given to Maureen throughout the week that are listed on their web site. She may receive special messages in parts over several days especially before a feast day celebration on the grounds. It is critical to know that to date *no single message or series of messages given at Holy Love has been described or singled out as contrary to Holy Scripture, faith or morals or Catholic Church doctrine, by any individual or group or church authority* (emphasis added).

Holy Love Ministries is and continues to be a place of prayer, meditation and conversion. Its sole purpose is to bring as many people as possible to full belief in God and to prepare them to witness to its truth through daily living.

The good news is that regardless of attempts to discredit the Ministry, Holy Love thrives, growing larger by the months and serving believers constantly through their web site and special feast days. It is a place of miracles, as we will discover in the coming chapters.

∾

Message given to Maureen on March 6, 1997:

Blessed Mother is here. She looks exactly how she looks in the picture [of her] that she helped me draw two evenings ago. She says: *I come to you tonight under the title, 'Mary, Refuge of Holy Love.' I desire that you propagate this image. Through modern technology it can be enlarged and hung prominently in our prayer center. Dear children, pray with me now for the conversion of all sinners.*

Dear children, please know and understand that many and particular graces will come to you through this image. It is my desire that you make this title and this image known.

Dear children, this is truly an alpha and an omega in the life of My Mission. It is the beginning of a new life in a new prayer center where many miracles and favors will be witnessed. It is the end of My Mission's exile. Tonight I am blessing you with My Blessing of Motherly Love.

FIVE

CALLED TO SERVE

The ministry of Holy Love has been blessed with the hard and difficult voluntary work of individuals who have been profoundly touched and transformed by the messages so much so that a select group now work full time for the ministry. Such sincerity and dedication maintains the accomplishment of Holy Love to be a place of profound faith.

These people who skillfully administer the services of the Ministry are extraordinary people who uprooted former lives to come to the area of Holy Love and dedicate their professional skills. Each one felt personally called to come to be an integral part of the Ministry. Without these extraordinary children of God, things would not run nearly as smoothly as they do at the site.

While there are many volunteers who do a wide variety of daily service on the grounds of Holy Love Ministries, we focus on the stories of Joan and Bob Topazio, Mary Ann Augustine, Laura Garcia, and Maureen's husband Don Kyle as key members of the extraordinary volunteers at Holy Love. Their stories of conversion and service actually represent those of all of the volunteers at the ministry.

We begin with the first-hand witness of Joan and Bob Topazio, both of whom serve many roles vital to the daily maintenance and operation of the ministry. It did not take long on my first visit to Holy Love to discover that the leadership of Bob was the "glue" that held it together and assured that things ran smoothly from the daily chores to orchestrating the special feast days. Don Kyle was astute enough to recognize exceptional management talent and to put him in the position of literally overseeing all aspects of the Ministry. It only adds credence to their account as to how they came to be part of the Ministry.

Here is the story of Bob and Joan. It is a story with interchangeable witness from each of them:

JOAN: It began as any other ordinary day and progressed to one of the most extraordinary days of my life. The morning chores were done. It was almost time to leave and pick up my daughter from school. I had just enough time to run out and get the mail. As I pulled the mail out of the mailbox I noticed that a favorite magazine had come. I loved the photographs of Medjugorje in this particular subscription and I was eager to see them.

Entering the house with the mail, I dropped everything on the table – except for the magazine. I fanned the pages quickly to preview the photos. What occurred from that point to the present day still leaves me in a state of profound amazement. A spectacular journey begins: I fanned the magazine pages quickly and satisfied my eagerness with a glimpse of the photos. I knew I was out of time – I had to leave.

I dropped the magazine on top of the pile of mail, grabbed my pocketbook and headed for the door. The minute I placed my hand on the doorknob an electric shock sensation surged through my entire body. I tried to pull my hand off but it was absolutely glued to the knob. I couldn't move. The sensation escalated immediately to the feeling of ice cubes rushing through my body – followed by a burning fire sensation. This occurred quickly and with intensity, as if Niagara Falls was ripping through me.

At the height of this experience I heard a voice clearly say, "**You need to go there.**" The sensation gradually subsided. I pulled my hand off the doorknob, which I hadn't been able to do since I took hold of it. This physical episode was absolutely riveting – like nothing I had ever experienced before.

The minute I took my hand off the doorknob my entire being was pulsating with an intense desire to go there. "I need to go there. Yes, I need to go there!" I said this over and over again out loud as I was regaining my equilibrium. Then it struck me: "Where?" "Where do I need to go?" I had such an intense desire to go there – but I had no idea where.

Instinctively I knew--the magazine. I walked over to the magazine – picked it up – opened it – read the very first thing I laid my eyes on, which was: "Five Steps to Holy Love."

I knew without a doubt – without any hesitation – this was where I had to go. The desire was overwhelmingly intense. I didn't know why. I just knew I had to go.

When my husband came home from the office I shared my story. After listening he was convinced that I was crazy. He did however agree to the trip.

BOB: At that time I was at the height of my career with a serious senior management job for an international Company. I was a good husband, a cradle catholic, a Eucharist minister etc., who knew and loved his wife. I tried to understand and finally agreed to investigate.

JOAN: Months later we made our first trip to Holy Love in Seven Hills, Ohio. I learned all that I could on this first trip about the beginning of the Ministry and the Messages. After our return home, I prayed for discernment, consulted with a friend who was a priest and carefully read the Messages.

BOB: During subsequent trips we observed many beautiful and astounding phenomena. Being the rational businessperson I would go and participate with our children, however being male I needed to be on reserve. Therefore as an example I would pray the rosary and walk around the perimeter of the field with only one foot in the door.

JOAN: On one early trip we prayed the rosary in a park. There were about 500-600 people. Just as we were finishing the rosary, a magnificent luminous cross suddenly appeared in the sky. The crucified head of Jesus appeared in the center. The crucifix was enormous. After a few minutes it dissolved and seemed to fall on all of us.

It was on this particular pilgrimage that my heart was flooded with affirmation that all that had occurred up to this point was real and true. Holy Love had to be a part of our lives for reasons unknown to me, except for the obvious: that we all need to love God and neighbor as self - which is Holy Love.

After the rosary was completed an invitation was extended to all present. If you wanted to speak and/or pray with the visionary Maureen, simply get in line. I marveled at how fast this line formed. Just about everyone rushed to get in line. I couldn't. I thought – how could I possibly approach someone who just received a message from Heaven. I felt very inadequate, but determined to honestly engage in some self-effacement when I returned home.

BOB: Our Blessed Mother has all the patience in the world and continued to work on me. I never resisted, yet did not commit. For nine to ten years we would regularly come to Ohio, alternating with driving and flying. We would come on as many special feast days as we could. Over time I began to realize that I no longer resisted and embraced what was happening. I have always lived in trust and accepted this as a grace. However, Heaven had more in mind for me.

JOAN: We did all that we could to promote Holy Love and spread the messages. We sponsored Maureen and some of the Holy Love staff to come and speak to people in our area. I thought that this was what I was being called to do – promote Holy Love. I did not realize that this was only the beginning of the total scope of Heaven's invitation.

When Maureen came for one of the conferences, we all had dinner together. We started to talk with each other – and with each response I came closer and closer to falling off the chair. When is your birthday Maureen? December 12th on the Feast of Our Lady of Guadalupe. Oh, wow, my birthday too. Oh, you have a Katie; our daughter's name is Katie—and so it went, the beginning of a wonderful friendship not to mention commonalities that were mind blowing.

Years later, as Bob and I were driving somewhere, out of the blue he said, "I think I'm going to take an early retirement and we should move to Ohio."

Well, I could have fallen right out of the car at that point. Needless to say – I was beyond shocked. He was vice-president of a very well known corporation and enjoyed his work very much.

BOB: It was time…Heaven can be very forceful and by being open it all began to come together.

JOAN: In the fall of 2005 Bob did resign his position and take an early retirement. We decided that when we visit Holy Love in the spring, for the Feast of Divine Mercy, we would take a few extra days and explore the towns in the area and access the real estate market.

We arrived about a week before the event. After checking into the hotel, we drove around to familiarize ourselves with the towns around the Shrine. That evening Bob went online to do a little research on getting to know the local communities. He put in North Ridgeville and turned totally white. I responded quickly with, "What's the matter?" He said, "Well, let me read the first line here for you – 'North Ridgeville was settled in 1810 by early settlers from Waterbury, Connecticut.' Wow! We were both surprised because we were from Waterbury, Connecticut.

Needless to say, we decided the next morning to explore North Ridgeville. We stopped at the shrine first. We pulled out of the property, taking a right and then a left. As we were going over a bridge I saw construction cranes and heard construction noises. I suggested that we turn around and check it out. Bob agreed.

We took a fast left on a little street to turn around. As we turned around and came back to the stop sign – I happened to look up at the street sign. "Wow!" I said to Bob, "You think last night was interesting with the town, check out the name of this street." The name of the street we turned around on was, Hedgerow. We live on Hedgerow in Connecticut! We thought that this was kind of amazing. But as I was thinking about it I remembered what a priest I knew would always say: "There is no such thing as a coincidence; everything is a God-incidence."

We arrived at the construction site, which happened to be a new, gated community for people over 55 years of age. The model homes were opened so we thought that we would tour them, just out of curiosity.

The agent was very personable and informative. She definitely had our attention. We spent the entire afternoon talking and carefully evaluating each model. We left very tired. I was thinking that we had a lot to think about and discuss after we returned home. My head was spinning at this point and I needed to immerse myself in prayer and Divine Mercy weekend, which were only a few days away.

That evening in the hotel room, to my complete amazement, the Blessed Mother appeared to me as Our Lady of Sorrows. I thought at first it was my imagination, so I repeatedly looked away, only to turn my head and see her again and again. I did this five or six times before I realized she really was there. She did not speak. This was significant for me as I have a devotion to the Sorrowful Mother and always go to the Sorrowful Mother Shrine first when on the property at Holy

Love. Bob was not in the room when this happened. I planned on sharing it with him the following day.

The next morning my head was spinning because it seemed as though the pace of everything was supersonic and the signs given were astounding and could not be ignored. I was still absorbing everything that had occurred. It was a Friday and I wanted to shift my focus on Divine Mercy and spend some quiet time in reflection and prayer.

With the intent of slowing things down so that we could review and discuss all that had happened, I said to Bob at breakfast, "So, we are going to go home and think about all this, right?" He responded, "No, I think after breakfast we're going back and give them a check for that house." Well, so much for reflection and slowing up the train. He was right.

BOB: I clearly realized that my entire career and skill path had directed me to this decision. My skills would be better used and needed here at Holy Love. Little did I know.

JOAN: We both knew in our hearts that Heaven could not have made it more clearly to us. We were being invited to come to Ohio.

We bought the house that day. We went back home and sold our house and moved to Ohio. We offered our gifts and talents to the ministry with a contentment and joy that really can't be explained.

Holy Love, the place and the spirituality, is one of those precious pearls of incalculable value. There isn't a day that goes by that I don't marvel at this special invitation from Heaven and thank our Blessed Mother and Jesus with all my heart.

BOB: Yes, it was and is the right decision. I often tell people that there is a special peace you feel when you cross the bridge into Holy Love. After all these years I continue to experience daily this peace. Trust and be open to Heaven's calling. If you come here, you might be just as surprised and blessed as we were and are, each day.

MARY ANN AUGUSTINE

I had been a fallen away Catholic, away from the Church for 30 years. I was first married in the Catholic Church in 1969, divorced in 1977 and remarried outside of the Catholic Church in 1982. I led a very active life as a registered nurse and co-owner of a business in Indiana.

Sunday, May 22 1994, I had returned home late in the evening from a state business meeting for women. My husband, shortly after my arrival, handed me a booklet and said he had found it in the back of our Church. It was unusual in that we went to church once in awhile because of my son and his Catechism classes, but we did not partake in the Sacraments. He said kind of jokingly that Blessed Mother was appearing in Ohio.

My response was great surprise and wonderment. I took the booklet from him and stayed up late that night reading the whole thing. That booklet was about Holy Love Ministries and messages from Mary to the visionary Maureen Sweeney-Kyle.

The messages took my heart away! All I could think of was that I had to go there. The only free day coming up was the following Sunday, May 29, 1994. I asked my husband if he would go with me, but his answer was, "No way!" So then I asked my 23-year-old son and he said he would travel with me.

We arrived at the House of Prayer in Seven Hills, Ohio (before the Shrine was moved to Eaton Township) just in time for a rosary service. We came at a very special time because we (a group of about fourteen pilgrims) were told that Our Lady would arrive while we were praying and would walk among us in the room. Just before she arrived, honestly, I saw a silvery cloud roll in through the large living room window. Then it was announced she was with us. I know it is not important to always see and feel things, but I truly did feel her awesome presence. I was so joyful during the whole rosary and my joy stayed with me even when I arrived back in Indiana that evening. My son felt the same way.

After the rosary, two wonderful volunteers, a married couple, gave us a little tour and took us to the Maranatha Spring. We washed our faces with the water, blessed ourselves with it, prayed and took a bottle of it home with us. When I arrived home, I put the bottle of Maranatha water next to my kitchen sink and went to bed.

The next day my son went back to college, my husband went to work and I was home alone. I walked up to the kitchen sink, took the bottle of Maranatha Spring water, sprinkled the water on my fingers and blessed myself. At that moment I found myself in a dark cloud as if the whole room disappeared. I felt a sharp pain in my heart and then I heard a voice. The voice said, (I'll never forget the words) "I have given you the greatest gift I could give my children, the gift of my Son in the Holy Eucharist. And you, through your own fault and your own sins, have lost that gift."

I tell you, I was in such pain and sadness. I sat down on the living room couch and cried and cried for most of the day.

When my husband arrived home from work, I was still sitting on the couch. I just said to him, "You know, we need to get our first marriages annulled and then get our marriage blessed in the Church." By the look on my face he could tell something happened, but not sure of what. He just said, "okay."

The next day I went to a priest to get the annulment process started. We received our annulments three years later.

Getting back to the story, after my first pilgrimage to Holy Love and my illumination of conscience from blessing myself with the Maranatha Spring water, I made a trip again in two weeks for the Blessed Mother's first message to the world on June 13th, 1994. When I returned to Indiana from this pilgrimage, I found myself going deeper into prayer. The rosary meditations had deeper meaning for me. Shortly after that trip, I was walking up my driveway after picking up my mail and was praying the rosary and was very deep into prayer. All of a sudden I felt this huge presence towering over me. I could not see it, but felt it and heard it. It roared and hissed at the same time and sent the biggest chill up my spine. I looked around the land and could not see any snakes or mountain lions or panthers or whatever. When I got into my house, I sat on the couch, still quite startled, and realized that it was Satan and he was angry because I was changing. He thought he had me and now was losing me. Whew! A horrible revelation!

Not long after that, I kept hearing in my heart that I was to work for Holy Love or to live a religious life. I wasn't used to listening to my heart, so I kept dismissing this inner voice. After about a year or so, one night while in bed I heard Blessed Mother call my name. I knew it was her because of her distinct voice. It was melodic and sweet. I've never heard a voice like that on earth. I turned over in bed and hid my head under the covers fearing she was in my bedroom. I kind of figured I was getting a confirmation of this inner voice. Still the inner voice continued, so I said, "Jesus, if this is what you want from me, you are going to have to hit me over the head, because I don't get it."

Heading into the third year, Our Lady asked Maureen to start having healing services every first Friday of the month. I came to the first service, which was May 2, 1997. I came to sit in for my mother who was diagnosed with cancer in February and given three to six months to live. Maureen prayed with me and said Jesus said to spray my mother with Maranatha Spring water. I was happy with that answer and then Maureen went on to the next person, then turned around, looked back at me, came back, made a fist and went knock, knock, knock on my forehead and said, "Jesus wants to know why you are reluctant to do His will?" I just laughed and said, "OK".

So, I moved to Ohio March 18, 1998. I've volunteered and worked here ever since. I still have the same peace and joy in my heart that I've had since my first visit on May 29, 1994.

Truly, I've lost my desire to go anywhere else in the world. I just want to live and work for Our Lady. I am happy! Holy Love is truly a bit of Heaven on earth, a respite from the world.

PS. My mother had two cancer sites and was in the last stages. She lived two years and three months after I sprayed her with the

Maranatha Spring water, as Jesus asked. But the greatest thing was that she was away from the Catholic Church for at least 50 or more years. She converted in the last few months of her life and was able to have a Catholic burial. And my time with her during her final week of life was so beautiful – much prayer, reconciliation, and mutual exchange of love.

Of course, there is much more to this story, but the best thing I can say is that the joy and peace of my first visit has never left my heart.

LAURA GARCIA

Laura is a translator for the Spanish-speaking pilgrims who come to Holy Love Ministries. She has been translating for 12 years. In addition to this busy job, she is also in charge of the propagation of the Confraternity of the United Hearts, as well as the distribution of the messages in Spanish. However, as important as these other duties are, Laura's central responsibility is management over the production of the Rosary of the Unborn. She arranges all steps in the production of the rosaries, overseeing the assembly and distribution. More than 15,000 Rosary of the Unborn rosaries are shipped per month, with distribution occurring mainly throughout North and South America. Here is her story:

I was a cradle catholic, going through the rituals of childhood but not strong in the faith. I went to church sporadically, but never really prayed the rosary or other prayers. In other words there was no

God in my life. I went to public schools, not Catholic ones and therefore, I had no training or instruction in my faith.

I got married at the age of 22. My new husband Armando was very religious and had attended Catholic schools. Soon, I influenced him to go the other way. Before long, neither of us was attending Mass. This state lasted for nearly ten years.

One day a friend invited Armando to a three-day religious retreat for males only. I was very upset that he wanted to go and since he was always working he had little time for the family. I was very upset and even more when I was asked to bring some kind of bakery goods to the retreat. I did not want to. I did not take anything.

On the last day of the retreat, there was a big celebration and the men were supposed to give their personal testimony. I listened to all of them and was then shocked when I heard my husband Armando. Later that week, he went around and knocked on all of the doors of the neighbors and asked forgiveness. He had always had a bad relationship with my mom and he even asked her for forgiveness. It was unbelievable how he had changed and I was deeply touched.

Soon after that retreat, we started going to Mass together. Somehow I felt a sanctifying grace that had come over us since the retreat. Shortly afterwards, they did a retreat for women. At first I said no, but having seen the changes in Armando, I felt I had to go. I accepted and went. Armando prayed to God: "You need to touch her heart if you want something from me. And send her the grace of conversion."

I clearly began to understand all of it. Jesus was there in the Blessed Sacrament and the tabernacle. I thought the rosary was only for certain occasions but soon found it could and should be prayed for everything. I felt the need to confess my failures. I realized how bad my life had been before all of this had happened, which was in 1997. Our lives changed. Everything was new: the praying of the rosary, Holy Mass –everything. Finally I asked Jesus to help me love his mother.

Armando was asked to teach children about the Church, and then I knew I had to give something back to God for what He had given me. I got involved in teaching and feeding the hungry breakfast. I started to give away rosaries and taught people how to make them and then give them to others.

In 2003, we met a priest who knew about Holy Love Ministries. He told us all about it. He wanted us to go with him to a conference in San Antonio, Texas for a conference where he was a speaker. It was there that we met Maureen and Don. I touched the Maranatha water and saw a power point presentation about the site and I immediately wanted to go there. Eventually they put me to work and I have been doing so ever since.

I started bringing groups to Holy Love from Mexico. I brought around 30 at first then nearly 300. I knew that God's grace was in all of this. It was not possible for me with my limitations. Today, I help with the praying of the rosary by doing a part of it in Spanish and also in translating the messages Maureen receives.

We have never been happier in our marriage and in our lives.

DON KYLE

Without the steady hand and solid faith of former police officer Don Kyle, there is question as to where Holy Love Ministries would be today. The same applies to the key people who joined the Holy Love Family in the beginning years and whose testimony is included here.

The ministry would have in all likelihood collapsed under the heavy attacks of skeptics and the hierarchy of the Cleveland diocese of the Catholic Church without the crucial leadership role of Don Kyle and by these faithful servants. That is a fact.

Don Kyle was born in Chicago, Illinois but moved to Cleveland, Ohio at a young age. He was an outstanding athlete, the "golden boy" at his high school. He spent two years of military service in the Marines.

In 1985 Don took early retirement from the police force and moved to Florida. During one period of his life, Don went 17 years as a fallen away Catholic. Somewhere along the way, he was talked into going to a Catholic a retreat renewal and during the sessions, he realized how much he missed his faith.

The "rest" of Don's story was covered in the previous chapter. The bottom line is he has undertaken the leadership role at Holy Love to assure that it continues on as the Blessed Virgin and her Son Jesus desire.

So there you have it. These special stories give credibility to the call of Holy Love Ministries, which is to "feed the sheep" as Scripture puts it. Without such dedicated leadership, who knows if it would have lasted as long as it has and accomplished so much in that time frame. Therefore, we can only thank God for the mission and the workers He called to lead it.

However, all was not roses along the way—there were thorns as well as we will see in the following chapter. It underlines the fact that the success and continued good fruits produced by Holy Love Ministries were not accomplished without crosses.

~

(Maureen) Today, as I entered my prayer room, I saw a great Flame that I have come to know to be the heart of God the Father. I heard His voice say:

I am the Alpha and the Omega, your Creator, the Eternal Now. In Me, there is no beginning or end, only now.

Today your country celebrates Thanksgiving, and you have been telling Me what you are thankful for. But I am here to tell you what I give thanks for.

I am thankful for this Pope who supports the Tradition of Faith. I am thankful for the Remnant who clings tenaciously to the Tradition of Faith despite Satan's confusion and promotion of his agenda. I am thankful for this Mission of Holy and Divine Love, and for the spirituality of the United Hearts, which many have accepted despite Satan's lies. I am grateful for the many who continue to add their numbers to the Ministry here, even to the point of uprooting and moving here. I am thankful for the promotion of the

Rosary of the Unborn, and for the many lives that are saved because of it. I am grateful for the many rosaries, prayers and devotions offered at this Site.

My thanks come to earth bound up in Divine Love. I have the eternal desire that Divine Love will be the Flame that consumes the heart of the world.

—November 22, 2007.

SIX

OPPOSITION

This is a chapter I sincerely wish was not necessary in telling the story of Holy Love Ministries. However, it must be included as it is an integral part of the whole story of Holy Love.

The very core of Holy Love is about love, not controversy. Unfortunately, Satan rears his ugly head to disrupt when souls are being saved in such large numbers. And, what better way to disrupt such grace than from such an unlikely source as the local hierarchy of the Roman Catholic Church, of which Don and Maureen are devout members.

The question asked by Holy Love when opposition commenced was, why? The same question remains today, 30 years later when hard, undeniable proof comes from confirmed great spiritual fruits. Holy Love, despite such powerful opposition, is a successful ecumenical shrine that continues to brings souls to deep spiritual conversion.

Actually, it could be said that the intensity of the opposition, just as it is at Medjugorje, stands as a strong indication that what is occurring there is truly from God in that it is constantly under attack. Look at the centuries old ongoing attacks against the Church established by Jesus. It is always under persecution. As further food for thought, despite the opposition the Ministry grows and continues to bring people to spiritual conversion.

No one involved in the early days of Holy Love Ministries would have believed that the local diocese of the Roman Catholic Church would become its major detractor, a full-blown opponent seemingly determined to either control it or see to its demise. Unfortunately, it continues to be the major opposition to the Ministry, even though *no formal investigation of Holy Love by the Diocese has ever been conducted* as of this writing. To put it bluntly: Holy Love Ministries has never been condemned by the Catholic Church. It also has never been condemned by the Cleveland Diocese. However, in November 2009, the bishop of the Cleveland Diocese issued a formal "admonition" for Catholics advising them to stay away from Holy Love. The fact is, it is an invalid action since the Diocese has no jurisdiction over an ecumenical entity. Further, the decree of admonishment was reportedly issued based on an investigation conducted by the Diocese by a person or persons unidentified. When Don and Maureen asked the Diocese for a copy of the investigation and who conducted it, they were told the information was "confidential."

In order to be objective in writing the story of Holy Love, I contacted the Diocese via email in November 2015, informing them that I was writing a book on the Ministry and wanted to give the Diocese an opportunity to explain the business of the admonition, the claim of an investigation of Holy Love and a list of other related questions. I was told at that time that a response would be forthcoming to my questions. Two weeks later, after several emails inquiring when I might receive answers to my questions, I received a short note with an attachment of the same decree that had been issued in November 2009. In short, there would be no direct answer to my questions.

Once again there is the comparison between Medjugorje and Holy Love. When the Medjugorje apparitions began in June 1981 to the six Croatian teenagers, the local bishop Pavo Zanic could not stay away from the parish. He believed completely and went so far as to state publicly: "These children are incapable of lying!" Several months later, Bishop Zanic turned against the apparitions and became it fiercest opponent.

The change of heart toward the apparitions at Medjugorje by the bishop was allegedly due to a threat of jail by local Communist authorities if he did not stop his open vocal support of the apparitions. They feared this entire business of so-called apparitions was actually an insurrection by the dominant population of Croatians in the village. The bishop began caving in when a group of local priests added to the threat by telling him they would seek his ouster as bishop of the Mostar diocese if he did not stop his support and belief in the apparitions. Yet, Bishop Zanic was so frightened by the thought of ouster that he called Father Jozo Zovko, pastor of the Medjugorje parish at the time, to his residence and asked him outright: "How can I a bishop become a parish priest again?"

There is no similar reason for the bishop of the Cleveland Diocese to have asserted such an aloof, uninterested and dictatorial hand toward Holy Love. No one was threatening him with jail or demotion. In fact, the attitude toward Maureen lacked the basic elements of charity and respect, which as a member of Christ's Universal Church should be the expected when dealing with the faithful, especially from a respected leader. Rather, the attitude was one of skepticism and dismissal.

There was never a direct meeting between Maureen and then bishop Pilla when she first reported to the Diocese as the Blessed Mother requested to tell him she was having apparitions. Instead, the Diocese summarily dismissed her. Years later when the Ministry had grown and flourished, Pilla's successor, Bishop Lennon, would not meet with Don and Maureen or other representatives of the Ministry even though he proposed such a meeting. Each time, he would find reason not to attend and would delegate someone from the Diocese to take his place.

Bishop Anthony Pilla was serving in the office when Holy Love began. He would have a controversial reign as Cleveland bishop, with serious questions concerning the handling of the diocese finances; and a chillingly high number of priests (145) of the diocese allegedly involved in sexual abuse cases (Again, allegedly, more than 1,000 victims). He would resign his office in 2006.

Richard Lennon replaced Bishop Pilla. He continues to serve in the office as of this writing. His attitude toward Holy Love is the same as the former bishop. However, even after his office agreed that Holy Love Ministries was ecumenical and therefore not under the

Diocese, he issued the admonishment based on a so-called confidential investigation.

There is no intent here to disrespect the person of Bishop Pilla or Lennon or the office of the bishop. However, it is necessary to give all of the facts concerning the obvious opposition to Holy Love once it became what it is today.

The question is, why would a Catholic bishop issue an admonishment against an organization that is ecumenical? It leaves one puzzled. It is the equivalent of the Diocese admonishing a Baptist or Methodist church which suddenly begins a devotion to the Blessed Virgin Mary, starts praying the rosary and recognizes the true flesh and blood of Jesus in their communion services as being "Too Catholic!"

Here is the truth in this matter of the Cleveland Diocese that *invalidates* the published admonishment by the bishop. The status of the Ministry as an ecumenical entity was *formally acknowledged and accepted* by the Diocese in a July 1996 meeting with an internationally recognized canon lawyer (Nicolas P. Cafardi, JCD) hired by Holy Love Ministries. At that time they met with a member of the chancery, Father Ralph Wiatrowski. It was agreed during this meeting by both sides that Holy Love Ministries was indeed ecumenical and was not seeking recognition as a Catholic organization. It was also agreed that the Diocese would make a "no comment" statement to all outside inquiries about Maureen and Holy Love Ministries. That agreement has been broken on many occasions since.

Therefore, the Cleveland Diocese by its own admission has no jurisdiction over the Ministry. The decree sent out by Bishop Lennon has no validation; and, in fact, it violates the rights of Don and Maureen. Worse, Bishop Lennon informed the Vatican that he had conducted an investigation of Holy Love (if done at all, it was conducted without including Maureen or anyone from Holy Love) and felt that Catholics were being misled because so much of Holy Love follows Catholic teaching and prayers.

All who come to the site know that it is ecumenical; no one is being misled. The sign placed at the entrance of the site clearly states it is ecumenical, as does its web site.

The only conclusion seems to be that the continued harassment by the Cleveland Diocese is more about control and money than about faith and the salvation of souls.

The primary goal of Holy Love Ministry is to bring souls to spiritual conversion through the power of prayer. It comes through obeying the great commandment to love God with all our heart, our mind and our soul; and, to love our brothers and sisters in Christ as we love our selves.

How could anyone, much less a Catholic bishop, object to that?

∾

Message given to Maureen on February 24, 2015. Our Lady comes as Mary, Refuge of Holy Love. She says:

Praise be to Jesus!

I must make clear that the Remnant Faithful is comprised of all Christians - not just Catholics. The Remnant is the coming together of those who hold Christian moral values in their hearts despite the com-

promise of Truth in the world. You, dear Remnant, must make the effort to be united in the Truth, as Satan is uniting evil in untruth. If you do not answer My call to be united, you will be defeated. Do not oppose one another. Recognize the enemy and oppose him. That is why it is so important to distinguish good from evil.

To all leaders, religious and secular, I tell you, do not make social justice your goal. If you do, you ultimately condone sins, which call upon God's Justice. You weaken the morals of society instead of strengthening them. You are working to unite evil.

Catholics must be united in Church Tradition and not accept language which supports illicit change. Stand shoulder to shoulder in the Truth. Be accountable to the Truth, not to man.

My Son has sent Me with these Messages for the Remnant to unite everyone in the Truth. Do not look to some new definition of the 'truth'. Be courageous in your fight against untruth. Pray to recognize the enemy who always disguises himself behind some good.

Remember, I am your Protectress and your Mother. I love you.

SEVEN

WITNESS

There are so many incredible stories of conversion that have occurred at Holy Love that it is difficult for the book to choose from the many that have occurred there. For that reason, this is by purpose a long chapter. Personal witness is the most powerful spiritual conversion tool. Witness from visitors to Holy Love Ministries dot the walls of the special little chapels built in honor of God in His three persons, as well as those honoring saints and angels.

I have subjectively chosen those I feel that will give a wide variety from people of different cultures, religions, ages and character. Some of the stories are funny, some extremely sad; some are long while others are brief and to the point. My purpose was to let each individual contributing to the book tell their story in their own words whether it is directly from them or given to me in interview. There are even stories of animals being healed at Holy Love.

We begin with the story of **Jeffry Bail**, who grew up as a Protestant:

Jeffry was raised in a Protestant home and began taking church seriously at the age of sixteen. That is when, he states, he gave his life to Jesus. The young man was strongly influenced by the devout faith of his family and was determined to always have Jesus in his daily life.

As Jeffry began his life as a college student to study accounting, he remained active in church activities and was soon an associate pastor at a non-denominational church working with the youth. Later, as Jeffry went about his activities, he also joined a few civic clubs involved in charitable work and at one of them he met a Catholic priest named Father Fred. As much as he did not want to like the priest because he was Catholic, he soon discovered that this priest was a nice person and they eventually became good friends.

Even with his active church life, Jeffry felt an emptiness inside that he simply did not understand. One day while aimlessly wandering through a Christian book story, Jeffry found a book on the apparitions of Medjugorje (my first book *Medjugorje: The Message*). He began to read an assortment of other Catholic books. Things began to change for the young man and he soon felt he had to resign from his church for what he called spiritual reasons. It seemed the pastor of the church made a comment about Catholics that upset Jeffry, referring to them as "carnals" for eating the body of Jesus.

Jeffry soon went back to his learned profession of accounting. The love of God was still in his heart but he could not find the right place of worship where he felt comfortable. Sometime in 1997, he first heard about Holy Love Ministries. He read that it was a place of prayer and he excitedly thought, "That is what I need!"

A short time later, Jeffry planned a trip to the site with a friend. They were impressed with the place but he would later admit that he was shocked when the meeting began with the praying of the Catholic rosary. What? He thought; no way! While he knew more about Catholics and knew about the rosary, he had basically observed from a distance but had never participated in a rosary prayer. Soon, his feelings changed. The more he listened, the more he liked it. There was a structure to it and it began to make sense as he realized it was the life of Jesus with some parts being about His mother Mary.

Sometime after that first exposure to the rosary prayer, Jeffry said he "felt Jesus say to him, 'I need you to look at my Church!'"

Of course there is a lot more to the story, but to summarize, Jeffry simply added that before long, was studying the faith and shortly thereafter, he became a Catholic. He still makes frequent visits to Holy Love where it all began.

RUXANDRA ROFF

I came to U.S.A. from Europe in 1989. My husband, John, and I are both from the same country. We were born during the time that Communism was spreading. We went to school there and were educated in the way not to believe in God. This started from first grade and went all the way to college. We never went to church and we never missed it since we did not have any faith. When we came to this country we did not go to any church because it was something that we had never done.

Our first two children were born in the states. They were ages three and eight when I found out that a friend of mine was very sick and the doctors gave her a short time to live. My friend was thirty-three and the mother of three children. There was no hope for her and we were all very sad. In less then a month after this bad news, someone told her about Holy Love and she asked me to go there with her. I was not happy about this friend's request since I did not believe in God; however, because she was so sick I did not want to disappoint her. We went together in May 2000. It was on a Friday night and we arrived just in time for the evening rosary. We did not know how to pray it, but we were there.

As we were praying, there was suddenly an announcement that the "Blessed Mother" was now appearing to the visionary Maureen. During the time of the apparition, I had a very strange experience. My whole body was shaking in a way that had never happened before and I had no control over it. This made me wonder what was going on. On our return home, I told my husband about it and he believed me. We started to go to Holy Love with our children on Fridays but in my heart I still did not fully believe that God was real.

A few months later, on December 12, 2000, we went to the midnight rosary for the Feast of Our Lady of Guadalupe. The weather was very bad, a very strong wind and rain, and during the apparition everything calmed down and some celestial lights started in the sky and lasted for forty-five minutes. We were all able to see them and it was something that cannot be described, something supernatural.

When we left we could not even talk. I remember that everybody was quiet but from that moment on both my husband and I knew that God is real and we realized how we were brainwashed in school.

We started to go to the Catholic Church and we are still going to Holy Love every Friday at 7 P.M. for the rosary. To get to the point, we were converted and my friend that took me to Holy Love is still alive and never had any more problems with the condition that she was diagnosed with almost 15 years ago. Unfortunately she does not go to Holy Love any more and she was not happy when we joined the Catholic Church, as we were all Orthodox before.

Later on, I was praying to have more children and the doctors told me that it was too late because I was 47 years old. One day I talked to Maureen about this and she told me to drink the water from Maranatha Spring. This was in the summer of 2005. Nine months later we were blessed with a baby girl! Her name is Rafaela Maria and Maureen is her Godmother.

I was 48 years old when she was born and all of the doctors told me they had never seen that in their entire careers. None of them could believe it.

DREW DAVIS

As a young five-year-old child, I awoke once in the middle of the night crying in pain and clinging to my legs. Something was terribly wrong. I went into my parent's room and woke my mom, complaining of terrible leg pains. Upon seeing how my legs had become severely swollen, my parents rushed me to the emergency room of a hospital in Fort Wayne, Indiana.

The doctors in the emergency room analyzed my legs and began taking many tests. When the test results came back, they showed that I had tested positive in four out of five tests for rheumatic fever, as well as being one test shy for a diagnosis of juvenile arthritis. Without certainty in their diagnosis, the doctors could not treat my condition, but only treat the pain. They recommended that I be sent to Riley's Children's Hospital in Indianapolis, where more extensive tests could be done. After proceeding to take me to Indianapolis, my parents were met with the same undistinguished results.

Days, weeks, and months went by and finally my condition had reduced me to being wheelchair-bound. It got to a point where the doctors told my parents that there was very little chance that I would ever be able to walk again and that, in all likelihood, my condition would only continue to get worse.

It was at this point that my parents had nearly given up hope, until a friend, Maryann Augustine, told them about this place in Elyria, Ohio called Holy Love Ministries and Maranatha Springs.

At this point my family, who considered themselves Christians, rarely went to church or practiced their faith at all. But, they were desperate for a cure and had exhausted all other options, so they decided to make the trip and give it a chance.

When my parents and I arrived at Holy Love, they toured the grounds and walked to the field where the rosary was being said and they began to pray. If you know anything of the rosary, it is a repetitive prayer that takes a significant amount of time to complete. On this particular day, the temperature had reached the upper 90's. This, in combination with the unfamiliarity with the location and prayer, made my mom and dad very uncomfortable. To top it off, I began to complain that I was thirsty. To quiet me down, they gave me the water from the (Maranatha Springs) well, with no expectations, other than to quench my thirst and get me to calm down. Once the day was over, we headed back home. We were not sure what visiting the place would do for me, but still, we hoped something would intercede for my condition.

Over the next few days, something did happen. The swelling was going down and my pain was going away! When it was time to go back to the doctor for my next appointment, I was walking again and there was no sign that I was ever ill. The doctor took X-rays, more tests, and nothing negative showed up. The signs of rheumatic fever and the other illnesses had completely vanished, and the doctor could not explain this phenomenon. He told my parents that my condition was severe and did not understand how it had quickly gone away with no medical treatment at all. He ended by saying it had to be a miracle.

Now that I was completely healed from my wheelchair-bound state, my family began to go to church more frequently, actively participated and learned about their faith. Those that visit Holy Love are given the promise that they will receive a healing in either a physical, emotional, or spiritual form. We experienced all three and our lives have been forever changed.

TOM BALLINCINO

Tom tells us a story about his brother's dog being cured at Holy Love. He states that the dog was diagnosed with bad hips and that it would cost more than $3,500 to treat. The dog, a chocolate lab, was in great pain. Tom offered to take her to Holy Love where he felt she might be healed. He placed her in his van and drove to the site. She was yelping in pain and almost bit Tom as he tried to make her comfortable.

On arrival at Holy Love, Tom took the dog to the back lot of the site. He got some water from the spring and put it on her hips, asking Jesus and the Blessed Virgin Mary to please heal the dog.

Tom then picked the dog up and set her on the ground and she started running pain free. Tom says it was unbelievable in that she was running around like a little puppy. The dog is now 15 years old and is doing wonderful.

BETTY GILLIS

I have been associated with Holy Love Ministries for more than twenty years now. Angels of Maranatha is a satellite office of Holy Love (we established) operating out of Philadelphia, Pennsylvania. We have been bringing pilgrims to Holy Love since 1996. We also host an organization called Make it Known, which has retreats to promote the Holy Love messages.

I was raised in a holy Catholic family but stopped going to church at the age of 17. I had a pious mom, very devoted to the rosary and always in prayer for us.

In 1994, I was diagnosed with a spinal cord tumor in my upper back that began to change everything in my life. I was married and had a child, a little boy named Steve. They removed the tumor but there were so many complications and they thought I would not live. I was ICU for 30 days. The pain was so bad that I was praying to die. One morning I woke up and saw three angels at the end of my bed. The one in the middle was shaking his head no and I knew that it meant I would live. However the doctors thought I would never walk again.

While still in rehab, I realized my husband could not properly raise our son due to his own drug lifestyle. It was then that I prayed to God to let me walk again so I could take care of my son. Soon after, we were divorced as my husband stayed on drugs. I was on a morphine pump. I prayed to walk.

I went home in a wheelchair and soon lost my joy. Later I found out that my sister was part of a group getting messages from an alleged visionary named Gianna. My sister had been to Medjugorje and later I sent a rosary there hoping for healing but no change. When it was returned, I prayed on it and the silver wire of it turned to gold.

Some time later, I learned of Holy Love and immediately I wanted to go there. My son said he would go with me, as it was a six-hour drive. We got there on May 5, 2000, and the first thing we did was the Stations of the Cross, which I wanted to do in my wheelchair; I had regained some walking but still needed it for distance. Then it was decided that I could not go because of the rocks on the trail. Shortly thereafter someone came in a golf cart and said she would take us. I was then able to walk all of the stations. I knew I was doing good but not the realization of the whole thing. I realized I was away from faith, but I could not take it all in at once.

My son was walking all around the place. I soon realized that I did not need to be in the wheelchair. I was in shock but I started thinking about my life, my history of drugs, and alcohol, my addiction and through it all, no church--just a party girl. A little later, I headed back to our hotel. I kept waiting to feel the pain and realized there was no pain during the whole day.

On our drive home I was on a high from the disappearance of the pain. I felt that maybe I was supposed to move to Holy Love and then I thought: Are you nuts?

My second visit to Holy Love Ministries was in August 2001 and this time, I drove myself there. It was August 4, and only a few people were there. That evening during the praying of the Sorrowful Mysteries, 1 looked up at the Sacred Heart statue and saw Jesus come out and float down and stare at me. I told Maureen about it and she said that's nice. What a grace!

That night I had a dream and the Blessed Mother said to me, "I want you to sell your house, move here and work for me." It was four o clock in the morning and I was wide-awake; it was so clear but crazy. I went home and I started to tell people about the dream and Our Lady wanting me to move to Holy Love.

It was not easy. Steve was just starting high school. I tried to talk to our priest about all that had happened to me but soon it seemed he started to avoid me. Nevertheless, I started going to Mass regularly and to confession and soon realized a full conversion. I remembered my promise in the hospital asking God to heal me so I could take care of my son. I now asked if this was His call. Blessed Mother, I prayed, make it happen.

I decided we were moving to Cleveland. My husband had divorced me and out of the divorce I received enough money to pay for our house. Now I knew I needed to downsize. I returned to Holy Love and said something to Maureen about moving here. I told her I had put the house on market; it sold almost immediately. Maybe it's a coincidence but the realtor was Catholic! I just knew I needed to work here. I prayed on it and six weeks later, my legs were stronger and I started going to daily Mass. One day Don Kyle told me that Mother Mary had a message for me. Really, I thought? Maureen got the message, and Our Lady said: "This is what I want Betty to do: Collect food, clothing and religious articles for the poor. And also use it for missions and prisons. I will give her the grace to do this."

Of course, I did what she asked me to do. We set up a Life Mission Center, which included abortion and pregnancy counseling.

Today, my health is still filled with pain, but I am doing things that I could not believe I could do. My son Steven went to Afghanistan and later joined a special charity walk to raise money for the Wounded Warrior Charity. I walked the whole thing and did it without too much pain.

That is my story and I continue serving at Holy Love.

MARY ANN MORALES

I am the youngest of four children. We were raised and educated in the Catholic faith including college. Holidays were spent with cousins and our "Reverend Uncle" Msgr. Mooney—a.k.a Uncle Pear. He would come and celebrate mass in our dining room. On occasion my mother's cousin, Fr. Joe Dirvin would visit us too. He was responsible for the canonization of Mother Elizabeth Seton and I recall him visiting or calling my mom and telling her the news of the cause of Mother Seton.

My formative years were very happy and I decided to attend Merrimack College in Massachusetts to pursue a B. S. degree in marketing. The goal was a career in pharmaceutical sales because I enjoyed the challenge of sales, and had a great interest in biology.

Uncle Pear was a friend of the CEO of a large corporation, which had a grocery and pharmaceutical division. With my uncle's help I landed a job in the grocery division where I worked for seven years before jumping into the women's health division. My job was to increase our market share of "women's health" prescription drugs of contraceptives.

Little did I know that during my training in female healthcare that I was being brainwashed into a mentality that views women as objects, and a mentality that treats fertility as a disease. It promoted the idea that women could not be trusted to take care of their own fertility or make prudent decisions regarding pregnancy, so we had to do it for them.

The marketing included the idea that the birth control pill was the panacea for all women's health issues: bad cramps, take the pill; irregular bleeding, the pill; acne use the pill; moodiness, take a stronger pill and so forth. Part of my job description included calling on Planned Parenthood and abortion clinics.

I was very content in my job, accumulating stock options and making lots of money. However, at home, things weren't so good. Mom was diagnosed with breast cancer, and I was suffering terribly with endometriosis. Endometriosis is called the silent sentence. It is an overgrowth of the lining of the uterus that attaches itself in the pelvic region rendering a person infertile and autoimmune. At this particular point in time I was misdiagnosed for this disease for 13 years. Doctors prescribed the pill to get rid of my pain. No diagnosis was ever made.

One day I called on a customer (ob/gyn) of mine who was suffering from infertility. Her name is Mary Anne. While I was waiting to speak with her, I noticed a book on her desk called *Holy Love, The Remedy and the Triumph*. She told me that she purchased that book at a place in Ohio where she went to pray for a child and then suggested I visit there because she knew my mom was ill with cancer. This peaked my interest as I was devastated by my mom's illness and was ready to do anything to help her. So I went there with my niece to pray for my mom's healing.

Nothing happened.

Being a sales rep, I convinced my extended family to return to Maranatha Spring and Shrine to pray for my mom. Subsequently my mom underwent a mastectomy, went into remission, but the cancer had returned into the liver and bone. After the trip, my mom's liver cancer disappeared and the bone cancer was under control. It was in short, a miracle. Mom came to Maranatha to thank the Blessed Mother. My mother passed away two months later surrounded by her family with the scent of roses emanating from the inside of her oxygen mask and also lingering in her room.

I'd love to tell you that I then returned to my Catholic roots and gave up selling the pill, but I did not.

The Blessed Mother was beginning to reel me back into the United Hearts because I had begun attending daily mass, reciting the rosary and the Consecration to the Flame of Holy Love everyday. Little by little the Blessed Mother was preparing Dr. Mary Anne and me for the "big reveal," which would come in the fall of 2002. Both of us were at Maranatha Spring and Shrine praying the rosary in the back of the old prayer center.

During the service we were asked to kneel because there was an apparition about to take place. Afterwards, Mary Ann Augustine (another Mary Anne!) came to the podium with the message that had just been given to Maureen. However, what we heard was not the actual message that had been given to Maureen that was being given over the microphone. What we heard was Jesus. He said to us: **"I know my lambs and my lambs know me. My lambs do not condone abortion, homosexuality, female priests, euthanasia, or any form of contraception, and if you do, I will not recognize you when you come into my kingdom."**

To say that we were stunned does not even come close to describing our emotions. We immediately began to argue right there who was more culpable for the sin of contraception. Yet we couldn't really put a finger on why it was so wrong other than "we are not supposed" to use it. And Jesus himself had just knocked us off the proverbial St. Paul horse and said we were in danger of losing our salvation! Wow!

My illumination of conscience came weeks after the trip to Ohio when I was at Adoration. The scales fell from my eyes, and the consequences of my job became crystal clear. It was all there before me, yet I couldn't see it. After connecting the dots of the reality that the pill can cause abortions, I realized that my weekly visits to Planned Parenthood caused many spontaneous abortions as well. Some physicians will use the pill as a form of a morning after pill to induce abortion. I was calling on these doctors giving them extra samples for this purpose. I considered myself pro life. However, this realization bought me so much pain and heartache that I knew I had to change my life.

First stop: confession. When I first started selling contraceptives a priest during confession told me to stop; but he added, well if you aren't taking it, all is well. This trip I visited a different priest who listened and then forgave my sins.

On September 8, 2001 I married my husband, Jose Morales. We struggled with male and female infertility and decided to investigate adoption. Amazing things began to happen. After a visit to Maranatha Spring and Shrine, like clockwork a few months later we were blessed with a child. We had Elizabeth in 2003, Gianni was adopted in 2005 and Matthew Sean came in the fall of 2005. Our hands and hearts were full. In September of 2003, I finally left my pharmaceutical company to raise my children full time.

After that infamous St. Paul trip to Maranatha Spring and Shrine in 2002, Dr. Mary Anne boldly gave up contraception in her practice and adopted a natural system of fertility care called the Creighton Model of Fertility. But the story doesn't end there. In 2012, Dr. Mary Anne was forced out of her office space and had to restart her practice. This is where the thought that we are going to work together for the Lord thing comes into being.

Today, our business is growing to the point where we need more laborers for the vineyard. The highest compliment one can give is imitation. Today, one of my clients has become a fertility Care Practitioner like me, and two more of my clients who are physicians have boldly decided to practice medicine in keeping with Church teaching and will be educated on the Creighton Model. We are slowly changing the culture of medicine in our area one soul at a time.

When I look back over my shoulder, I realize that Dr. Mary Anne was right; our work is not ours; it is the Lord's work. My journey with the United Hearts has taken me to places I could never have imagined. And it all began at Holy Love Ministry along with my yes to the United Hearts.

T.M.

Cambridge, MA.

In May 2009, my father became very sick. It started with a problem in his lungs. My father kept getting worse each day. As the weeks went by, the seriousness of his illness increased. He had a severe form of inflammation in his lungs, which prevented him from breathing.

The doctors decided to put him on a respirator. This made him suffer even more and did not help at all.

My father became worse. He had many blisters on his face. His body was so swollen to the point of just about exploding. Each day the diagnosis was more disheartening as there was no hope for a healing. The doctors suggested removing the respirator from his mouth and placing it in his throat. They thought that might help. I felt that my father was going to die.

The doctors did this procedure. It was hard to watch and see my father suffer so much. I could see that he could not endure any more pain. His eyes were filled with tears. I watched him fighting for his life. He had openings in parts of his body because the doctors had put in drainage for the lungs so they would clean out. He went into a coma for more than two months. There was no improvement.

The doctors said there was absolutely no hope that my father would live and that there was nothing more they could do for him. In the moment that the doctors were telling me this, I just felt that God was going to give my father a miracle. I didn't know how, but I had trust. I told the doctors to remove the respirator.

The next day, a friend came to the hospital and brought me a small bottle of Maranatha Spring water from the property of Holy Love. With faith, we started giving my father drops of water with a hyssop, as he could not swallow due to his mouth being so sore from the tubes. In two days, we gave my father three bottles of the water. Several days later, the doctors removed the machine and said that he was going to die in 24 to 48 hours. They put him in a different room to wait for him to die. That moment never came.

Within the time frame the doctors had given my father to die, he instead started to get better. He began to breathe on his own and his strength began to return. In less than a month, he got his voice back and started speaking to us. His lungs were like new lungs and the doctors could not explain his sudden healing. They said it was truly a miracle.

I give infinite thanks to God and his holy Mother Mary.

B. N.

Haverstraw, NY

I am 15 years old and have had bad eczema all my life. I was born with it. It was so bad that I couldn't even open my hands without them bleeding. One look at my legs would make you want to cry. There were many days I could not go to school because my hands were bleeding so much. Holding a book or pencil was impossible. I went through lots of pain, suffering and medications; doctors, pills, creams, medicines and everything you could imagine.

My family and I went through so much in an attempt to heal my skin but nothing would work. I would still bleed and suffer.

I came to Holy Love many times with my family and each time we came we would receive new graces. We always prayed for my skin to be healed. We would put Mother Mary's tears on it from the Lake of Tears at the Sorrowful Mother Shrine and we would pray.

When I came to Holy Love for Divine Mercy Sunday on April 7, 2013, I told Jesus that if He wanted to heal me, I knew He would, and if He didn't, I would offer it up as a sacrifice for the Holy Souls in Purgatory.

I spent the whole day at Holy Love with my skin burning. It felt as if I were set on fire. By the time of the apparition in the field of the United Hearts, my skin was all red and bleeding. When it was announced for us to please kneel (the time of the apparition) I knelt down and closed my eyes. Right then, I knew something spectacular was happening. My breathing began to stop. I had multiple sensations on my skin where I had the eczema. I had never experienced anything like this before.

When I opened my eyes, the eczema on my neck and hands was different. By the time I walked to the bus, my forehead, ears and hands were totally clear!

I have nothing on my skin anymore. It is as if I never had it at all. All I have left are little scars. I think Jesus gave me new skin on Divine Mercy Sunday. I thank him every single moment. There is nothing He can't do!

Through all of these stories of witness, you have a sampling of the proof that comes with belief. There are literally hundreds of witness stories stemming from people discovering Holy Love. Each story serves as credibility of what is transpiring at this site.

As Jesus says in Scripture: **"You will know them by their fruits."** We will see more confirmation of the good fruits that flow from Holy Love Ministries in the next chapter as we review a collection of the messages given to Maureen over the years.

~

Message given to Maureen on January 1, 2014; The Solemnity of the Blessed Virgin Mary, the Mother of God.

Our Lady comes seated on a Throne. She is in white with gold ornaments on Her Mantle. She says:

Praise be to Jesus. Today, you honor Me under the title 'Mother of God'. I am the Mother of God, but also *the Mother of All Humanity. I am the Mother of all who esteem Me and pray to Me. I am also the Mother of all who have abandoned Me. I am the Mother of those who live in error, those far from their salvation and all who promote sin. My Immaculate Heart is the Chamber of Purification where souls can face illumination and conviction in the Truth. Not believing in the Truth does not change the Truth. Conviction of heart is a great grace in any present moment, and must be accepted for conversion of heart to take place. Therefore, as your Mother, I call each soul into My Heart as I tenderly and profoundly call you to realize the Truth of where you stand before God in any given moment.*

EIGHT

WORDS FROM HEAVEN

Just about everything contained in the book up to this point comes from or leads up to the actual words spoken to Maureen by Jesus, the Blessed Virgin Mary—even from God, The Father. There is also a limited cast of saints and angels. Little explanation is needed as the messages clearly speak for themselves.

Amazingly, there have been more than 30,000 messages given to Maureen since that fateful day in January 1985 when it all began.

Special messages are given for the feast days celebrated at Holy Love throughout the year. Quite often Maureen will begin receiving the specific feast day message days before the actual event. It will come in parts and is usually completed before the special day of celebration, or, during the praying of the rosary on that day. The complete message is then read to the crowd present for that particular feast day; and, it is always after the completion of the rosary even though Our Lady at times comes in apparition to complete the message during some part of the rosary prayer. The message is then read somewhere around midnight.

It goes without saying, that the messages given to Maureen are the most important element of Holy Love Ministries. They are the heart and soul of all that transpires there. The focus here is to bring attention to the actual words Maureen receives with each apparition of Jesus, Mary and the others from Heaven. I will primarily promote a segment of the latest messages given to Maureen during the year 2015. However, there are key messages that she recommended for the book and they will appear at the beginning of this chapter. There is no need to attempt to explain the meaning or the importance of one message or another. The meaning of each message essentially explains itself.

It is suggested that the reader take the proper time to read each message, even possibly reading one or two at a time and then taking time to meditate on its content. Remember, while the messages are given to Maureen, they are meant for everyone.

We begin with this powerful message given to Maureen on October 7, 1993 (Feast of the Holy Rosary):

Our Lady is here as Our Lady of Fatima. She says:
All praise, honor and glory be to Jesus.
Then She said:
Pray with Me now for all those souls who are spiritually apathetic.
We prayed. She says: *I desire very much that My priest sons universally accept the encyclical of My Pope, for it dispels darkness that has cast its shadow upon the Church.*

She has three rosaries [in her hands]. One does not have any beads; one has just a few beads, and the third rosary has all its beads. Our Lady then stated:

The one [rosary] *that does not have any beads represents the Rosaries that are never said. The one [rosary] that has just a few beads are Rosaries that are not prayed from the heart, and these two are the same as giving Satan power. But Rosaries that are prayed from the heart are a great, great weapon in My hands against all evil. Dear children, pray, pray, pray.*

Our Lady blessed us and left.

$\sim$

Message given to Maureen on July 19, 1999:

Jesus and Blessed Mother are here with Their Hearts exposed. Blessed Mother says:

Praise be to Jesus.

Jesus:

I am your Jesus, born Incarnate, King of Mercy and Love. My brothers and sisters, allow your hearts this night to be cleansed and renewed in the spirit of Holy Love so that I may use you to the fullest. Bring Me souls. Pray for the conversion of the world. We're extending to you tonight the Blessing of Our United Hearts.

$\sim$

Message given to Maureen on September 18, 1999:

Jesus:

I have come to speak to you about prayer, and in particular the prayer of the Rosary. I am your Jesus, born Incarnate. So many surrender to prayer without the sentiment of love in their hearts. This weakens the prayer, making it less worthy. Instead, bolster your prayers by recalling the love you have in your heart for Me and My Mother. This allows Me to pour the choicest graces upon you and into your life.

Prayer has a cumulative effect. I know ahead of time how many prayers will be offered for each petition. Therefore, you never know what just one more Hail Mary will bring. One Hail Mary said with a loving heart has the power to stop wars, bring nature into harmony with God's plan, convert an unbeliever, save a vocation, deliver a soul from purgatory, and change the future forever. Think, then, of the power of a whole Rosary said with love.

Satan knows that the Rosary is the weapon which will bring about his defeat. This is why he is desperate to discourage its use. Every time you recite a Hail Mary from the heart, the devil is weakened forever in some area and in some soul.

You must never be discouraged, then, in praying the Rosary. When your heart is most filled with distraction, understand the adversary is frightened of your prayers.

The Heart of My Mother is consoled by your efforts in prayer. She is most indebted to the ones who persevered in a regimen of prayer despite opposition. Make it known.

~

Message given to Maureen on April 27, 2014:
(This Message was given in multiple parts over several days.)
On Friday, April 25, Blessed Mother came and said: *Praise be to
Jesus.*

*I have come to preface My Son's public message so that all will thor-
oughly understand His Words and the message will have full impact.*

*My Son begins by calling all people into His Mercy. He warns that
souls must hasten to recognize the errors in their own hearts and see the
need of His Mercy or else experience His Justice.*

*The last part of His message addresses the Remnant Faithful. He
is now forming the New Jerusalem in hearts that cling to the Truths
of Tradition. He refers briefly to His Second Coming when He will be
seated on the Temple Mount. He refers to the Remnant as a holy nation.
It is a nation in hearts, not in any specific location.*

Meditate on these Truths of these times.

(3:00 P.M. Service)

Jesus is here as He is in the Divine Mercy Image. He says: **I am
your Jesus, born Incarnate.**

**As you gather to celebrate the Feast of My Divine Mercy, cel-
ebrate as well, My Mercy of Holy Love - the Messages and all the
graces attendant here at this site. Realize that Holy Love is My
Last Profound Intervention between the heart of the world and My
Own Most Mournful Heart. The next intervention, which I hold
back by merit of the prayers of the faithful, will be My Justice. The**

action of My Arm of Restraint is withheld by the Will of the Father. Only He knows the terrible hour of its release.

I come to strengthen and increase the Remnant and make firm their resolve in the Truth.

I tell you, solemnly, the conscience of the world has become convoluted due to the compromise of Truth. Evil is not recognized as evil. Sin is no longer recognized as sin. Therefore, people do not seek out My Mercy. They see no need of My Mercy. Yet, I tell you, My Divine Mercy is the world's last recourse of hope.

The gravest threat to mankind is not war or nuclear disaster, or even grave natural disasters. The biggest threat to mankind is his inability to distinguish good from evil. Thus, he continues to weaken his relationship with Me and to cease searching out My Father's Divine Will. This disconnect between Heaven and earth needs to be man's greatest concern and most urgent cause for correction. Herein lies the remedy for peace and restoration of prosperity.

Today, I come to make of you a new nation - a nation set apart from all others, a nation which is not bound by geographical borders, politics or economy. It shall be a nation like no other. It is destined to be a nation in hearts; hearts which embrace the Truth and live in Holy Love. This nation is formed from My Overflowing Mercy for souls. It will be governed by the Divine Will of My Father. He will show no favoritism; nor will He accommodate or pander to those in error. He will, at His Perfect Time, place Me in victory over all error and I will be seated on the Temple Mount. Then, you will be given the freedom to love Me openly and to pray whenever and wherever you desire.

Yes, I am laying today the foundation of the New Jerusalem in all hearts that live in Truth.

This holy nation - this nation of Truth that I speak of - is the Remnant Faithful. It is these tenacious souls who will form the foundation of the New Jerusalem. They have already begun to do so as they cling to Tradition.

All of the messages that begin this chapter were special recommendations by Maureen. I selected the next three due to the power of each message:

Message given to Maureen on January 2, 2014:

Jesus:

I am your Jesus, born Incarnate.

No one can be saved or come into Paradise outside of God's Divine Will. So it is, through and in this Divine Will, I come to offer the path of Truth, which leads you into the Light. If you pursue the Chambers of Our United Hearts, you will live in the Truth and obey My Father's Commandments. So it is, I offer you a roadmap to Eternal Joy - a Joy beyond all telling. It is easy to disbelieve and thereby discount what I offer, but disbelief does not free you of the responsibility to discover the Truth. Today, you are experiencing much snow in your part of the world. I tell you, some hearts are 'snowed under' by error. Holy Love must melt away the error and help them to begin their journey towards the Divine Will. Be the instrument, which melts the ice.

~

Message given to Maureen on January 4, 2014:

Jesus:

I am your Jesus, born Incarnate. There are those in the world today who seek to redefine Truth to appease the error that is in their own hearts. There are those in power who mandate the choice of sin. My Protection and Provision stand firmly in the face of every arrogance, that attempts to destroy Truth. If you wonder why I come to you repeatedly with messages in defense of the Truth, it is a sign to you that evil uses untruth to rise to power. Therefore, I am unrelenting in bringing the Light of Truth into the world. It is this Light which exposes evil. Do not allow your freedoms to be stripped away so that you must choose evil. Hold onto your right to be holy in a secular society. Those in power are in grave danger of choosing unwisely and cooperating with evil, and they do not recognize this danger.

~

Message given to Maureen on January 6, 2014:

The Blessed Mother says:

Praise be to Jesus. Dear children, I come, as always, seeking to place the rosary in your hands, for this is your defense against weapons of mass destruction and every diabolical plan. I seek to place Holy Love in your hearts so that you can be at peace and be saved. Do not be stubbornly complacent in acting according to My call to you. Do not use the excuse that it is 'okay' to disbelieve just as others do. Take the first step in faith by praying the rosary. I will give you the grace you need to believe. Every doubt is from Satan who does not want you to believe or to pray. When you pray the rosary, dear children, Satan loses power in your hearts and in the world. Do not allow these, My words to you, to go unheeded. Pray, pray, pray.

∼

Message to Maureen on January 1, 2015:

Our Lady comes all in white with sparkling lights around Her. Blessed Mother says, *Praise be to Jesus.*

Dear children, as today we begin a new year, I invite you to see it as an invitation to come closer to My Jesus and deeper into Our United Hearts. Allow this coming year to open upon new resolves to be holier and to live these Holy Love Messages from the heart.

Do not allow yourselves to be discouraged by unbelievers or by the apostasy all around you. You will be given many opportunities throughout the coming year to be examples of Holy Love to others. Use them. Be charitable to others in thought, word and deed. I will multiply your good and increase the grace in your hearts.

Change will become commonplace in the new year throughout the world. But, Jesus is your constant. Abide in Him. You can transform hearts through prayer. Therefore, have hope - always hope that change will bring good.

Dear children, I am blessing you.

~

Message given to Maureen June 27, 2014, Feast of the Sacred Heart of Jesus:

I am your Jesus, born Incarnate.

These are nefarious times - times when a far distant threat quickly becomes a present moment danger. These are times in which geographical borders have become obscure and distances between hemispheres are dwindling due to modern day technology.

Instant communication is at mankind's fingertips, and yet he neglects the most important communication - the one between his heart and My Sacred Heart. My Mother came as Protectress of the Faith to this seer, but this most appropriate title was deemed unnecessary. Yet, today, the faith has been pillaged by the compromise of Truth.

Certain grave sins are no longer considered sins. Rather, they are legal rights. The sanctity of marriage has been vandalized in an attempt to pander to 'special interest' groups. The life I create in the womb is under attack by those who do not see the new life as a human being. Even this Truth has been re-defined. These days, when so much is made of identification through DNA, do you not comprehend that the new life I place in the womb is human? You are killing human beings! Once again, I repeat what My Mother has told you. You will not have peace in the world until there is peace in the womb. Allow My Commandments of Holy Love to take dominion over your hearts before it is too late.

My Sacred Heart mourns for the compromise of Truth in the world today. This compromise opposes right reason, which discerns the difference between good and evil. If you cannot distinguish what is good and what is evil, your very salvation is at stake! It is this inability or unwillingness to recognize evil that has caused mankind's moral decadence.

I shed My Blood for your salvation. Mankind must shed the errors of his heart in order to choose this gift of his own salvation.

∼

Message to Maureen given on January 30, 2015:

The first step to living in Holy Love is to choose it. This choice may need to be made over and over throughout the day. Entrance into the First Chamber encourages this."

It is important that the soul determines the direction his thoughts, words and actions are taking him. Are they inspired by good or by evil? Certainly, it is clear that there are evil inspirations in the world today. It is also evident that evil is most often presented as good. The heart that does not fully accept this is easy prey for Satan.

Dear children, you must not be complacent, for Satan knows the best way to infiltrate each heart. He knows your weaknesses and your strengths. Please recognize him in every anxiety, every weakness of virtue and every discouragement. Read each Message I impart to you as though I am speaking directly to you.

I desire our hearts beat in unison in every present moment.

～

Message to Maureen on February 27, 2015:
Jesus says:
I am your Jesus, born Incarnate.
I wish to describe to you a good and worthy leader. Such a leader has the welfare of his followers first and foremost in his heart. He does not lead according to his own benefit. He does not allow power, reputation or love of money to control his decisions.

A worthy leader is a reflection of the Remnant Faithful as he practices the Moral Standards of Truth. The good leader has no guile - no hidden agenda, but is open and truthful in every endeavor. Therefore, he is trustworthy.

In the world today, there are few such leaders as I have described to you. Politics rules hearts and thus decisions. Honesty is synonymous with Truth. Truth bespeaks clarity - transparency - reality. Most in leadership roles today are concerned with themselves - their importance, reputation and climb to success. These are not the ones you should follow if you wish to follow Me.

～

Message given to Maureen on March 9, 2015:
Jesus says:
I am your Jesus, born Incarnate.
Please understand, the Remnant Faithful to which all are called is not an organization that a person signs up for and con-

ducts meetings to attend. With this Holy Remnant, one member would not recognize another if they passed on the street. There is no president, secretary or treasurer of this Remnant Faithful. Rather, the Remnant is in hearts - formed in hearts and a part of the heart. The Remnant Faithful is the belief in Christian morals, the Ten Commandments embraced by Holy Love and, if Catholic, the Church Tradition.

In the world today, what is concealed in hearts directs the course of human history. You see violence on the rise and terrorism becoming more of a threat. These things are products of the heart; but I come to you through these Messages to encourage and strengthen good in hearts. Good must be united and portrayed in the world in order to conquer the evil of these times. Evil has been in the world since Adam and Eve; but never to the extent as it is today. Modern technology has made it easier for evil to propagate its cause. Satan provokes good to oppose good and clouds the difference between good and evil.

The secrets of men's hearts are now being revealed. My call to righteousness, although Satan besmirches My call, is My Hand reaching out to humanity before it is too late. Grasp My Hand in Holy Love.

∾

Message given to Maureen on March 23, 2015:
Our Lady comes as Mary, Refuge of Holy Love. She says:
Praise be to Jesus.

You are living in times which are difficult to understand. These are times when Truth is elusive, especially to the proud of heart. The proud redefine Truth to suit their own agenda. I speak to their angels in an attempt to grant each soul - no matter his spiritual state - self-knowledge, which is salvific.

You must remember that error must be recognized in order to be corrected. This generation, however, has become spiritually blind. If I were to better define this blindness, I would say it is the inability to distinguish good from evil. This is a basic necessity towards each soul's salvation.

It is a grace not to be concerned with who agrees with you or who does not. In order to stand firm as a Remnant Faithful, you must pray for this grace. You must choose to please God and not man. Remember, always, God sees into each heart and knows your inner struggles. The Holy Spirit - the Spirit of Truth - will help you to find the Truth in each situation and give you insight into your own heart. Do not let pride obstruct the Truth of the state of your heart.

If you must correct another, do so without malice. Do not pronounce rash judgments on another, but in all ways be fair minded - not seeking your own advantage, but the Truth.

∾

Message to Maureen given on July 28, 2015:
Our Lady comes as Mary, Refuge of Holy Love. She says:
Praise be to Jesus.

You never receive the same grace twice just as you never are of-
fered the same present moment twice. There are always interior and
exterior circumstances, which affect and alter the grace of the present
moment. This is why it is so important that the soul does not cast concern
on the future. When the future becomes the present, so, too, will the grace
be there that is needed.

God's Provision is complete in every present moment. The grace is
given to succeed in that which God desires you succeed in and to support
you in trials and difficulties. Whereas people fail you, God's grace is a
constant! Respect what I am telling you and be at peace.

∼

Message given to Maureen on July 31, 2015:
Jesus is here with His Heart exposed. He says:

I am your Jesus, born Incarnate.

My dear brothers and sisters, please have confidence that your
prayers and sacrifices are helping convert the heart of the world.
They are weapons in My Hands, when offered with Holy Love.

Do not be discouraged.

Tonight, I'm blessing you with My Blessing of Divine Love.

∼

Message given to Maureen on August 2, 2015:
St. Joseph is here and he is holding the Baby Jesus.
St. Joseph says:

"Praise be to Jesus."

"My brothers and sisters, please realize that the role of the father in the household is definitive. It is a mistake for the father to try to be a pal to his children. The father's role is to lead spiritually and emotionally with authority and respect.

"Tonight, I'm imparting to you my Fatherly Blessing."

∾

August 15, 2015, **Solemnity of the Assumption of the Blessed Virgin Mary** (This Message was given in multiple parts over several days.)

Our Lady comes in white and gold. She says:

Praise be to Jesus.

She has tears glistening in Her Eyes.

I am happy My children have gathered here to pray at My Request.

I am responding with My Grace at this site as a fruit of the many prayers and sacrifices My children have offered here for the heart of the world. Please understand that Jesus does not call you here for My benefit but for the welfare of all humanity and, in particular, for each one who comes! It is not My Intention to impress those who oppose us with great numbers of people who flock here. Yet, I do pray for all to respond with love and expectant faith to My Invitation to come in pilgrimage and to witness My Presence here.

I will withhold nothing if you ask with Holy Love in your hearts. Remember, expectant faith does not seek proof, but believes in what it cannot control or make happen through human efforts. Expectant faith is the good fruit of trust.

God answers each prayer in His Way - in His Time.

Dear children, I have come, once again, to remind you of the precipice that the heart of the world is teetering upon. There are clearly two paths open to the future. One is the continued disregard for God's Will and the moral degeneration it leads to. The other is the desire to please God, keep His Commandments and pursue God's Will in every way. You must not wound the Mournful Heart of My Son anymore through the abuse of authority and the compromise of Truth. His Justice is already greatly antagonized and provoked.

If you continue to destroy life in the womb through the compromise of Truth, you will ultimately destroy yourselves and the world as you know it! The technology God has given you - DNA - proves you are destroying human life. Even those devoted to the intellect must concede to this Truth. The hope of this nation and of the world is not in man-made peace agreements, which are constructed upon untruth and guile, but in the reversal of abortion represented as a legal alternative to life.

Dear children, today I would like to describe to you a world without the horror of legalized abortion. In such a world, all life from conception to natural death would be respected. God's Will would, once again, take precedence over the free will of man. Great leaders - political and religious - would be born into the world instead of being sacrificed on the altar of abortion. There would be more respect for human existence; therefore, violent crimes would be drastically reduced. The difference between good and evil would be more clearly perceived as mankind would place God, once again, in dominion over the heart of the world. The Truth would come to light where it has laid hidden.

But these things cannot happen while the unborn continue to be sacrificed as in the days when I appeared at Guadalupe. Then, the world was uncivilized and barbaric. Today, it is no different except that you have had the privilege of knowledge between good and evil. Back in the days of Juan Diego, My Apparitions were accepted as true by the Bishop and many came to believe.

Here this is not so. Everything has been done - openly and behind the scenes - to discount Heaven's intervention at this site. A great miracle was performed at Guadalupe in the form of My Image. Here, it cannot be so because of so little faith. Even Jesus did not perform great miracles in His native town due to the lack of faith (Matthew 13:58). The miracles that abound here on an individual basis are not investigated and are summarily dismissed.

The execution of God's Grace is perfect towards each one's salvation. No one who comes to the property or reads the Messages** remains the same.

I have given you here at this apparition site all you need to believe and to convert. I call you into the Light of Truth. Do not persist in your quest for others to agree that this is from Heaven and authentic. Some, during their lifetime, may never recognize the Truth. In this persistence of disbelief, they have discouraged countless graces.

The great miracle that some seek as proof of the reality of Truth here is the spirituality given forth in these Messages and in the fact that this Mission exists despite all the calumnies, detractions and power plays against it. Each soul who journeys here will find what he needs -

a refuge from the foe - if he enters My Immaculate Heart. Individual miracles of conversions and healings will continue to abound. These will matter little on the grand scale in a world that does not even acknowledge the miracle of life in the womb, however.

I began this Message by describing to you the bounty of graces that come with expectant faith. I end by warning the world populace that you cannot continue in your lack of faith in Holy Love and expect God's Blessings upon your future. I am calling each of you back into God's Will where you will find peace and security. Your faith in Holy Love is your vehicle of salvation. These days it is challenged on all sides. Seek the protection of My Immaculate Heart by invoking Me under the title of Mary, Protectress of the Faith. That is the key to My Immaculate Heart. I will promptly defend your faith against the foe.

Today, My concerns reach far beyond this Ministry which has been so misunderstood, misrepresented and maligned. My Concern is for every one of My children adrift on a sea of abuse of authority and compromised Truth.

My Immaculate Heart must be the anchor that holds you to the Tradition of Faith. Sequential events will occur in the world, which will try to pull you away from the Truth; but I have come to protect your faith and shelter you in the Refuge of Holy Love, which is My Heart. Have recourse to me.

Dear children, today I invite you to be united with Me, your Holy Mother. Every day pray with Me, that the heart of the world recognizes the truth of the difference between good and evil. It is only in this way evil will be defeated in hearts and in the heart of the world.

I'm taking every petition into My Heart today and carrying it to Heaven and I'm blessing you with My Blessing of Holy Love.

Message given to Maureen on September 10, 2015:
Our Lady comes as Rosa Mystica. She says:
Praise be to Jesus.

Today I remind you that not all leaders are equally qualified to lead. The inadequacies in leadership stem from what is held in the heart. False virtue - that is virtue practiced to impress others - leads to compromise of the Truth. Such a one given to false virtue is most likely to safeguard his reputation at the cost of the Truth. He does not look so much towards the welfare of his followers as he does towards his own benefit."

Dear children, practice every virtue no matter the cost to self and look for this attribute in leadership. Do not support anyone given over to lies or confusion. They are unworthy of your loyalty. The truly virtuous leader will not redefine sin as a freedom. If you had just leaders in the world today, you would not have conservative and liberal divisions in the secular or religious world. Rather all would be one. There would be no confusion. Pray for all leaders that they realize their place before God.

~

Message given to Maureen on September 28, 2015:
I am your Jesus, born Incarnate.

Globalization - like anything - can be good or evil depending upon its purpose. If the purpose is to spread Holy Love worldwide, it is, of course, a noble cause. If however, the intent is towards a one-world government, this would pave the way for evil to rule the world. A one-world government, while it may be presented as a sound solution to many problems, makes it very easy for people to be manipulated and deceived if the chosen leader is evil.

Leaders in past history may have been very popular and yet held evil agendas in their hearts which did not surface until it was too late. Stay grounded in Holy Love. Let Holy Love be your barometer of what is good and what is potentially evil. The grace of My Mother's Heart will not abandon you.

∽

Message given to Maureen on the Feast of the Holy Rosary, October 07, 2015 (This Message was given in multiple parts over several days.):

Dear children, thank you for answering My call to come here on the Feast of the Holy Rosary. If I could summarize the thirty years of Messages given this visionary, I would say they are all contained in the rosary. Every mystery is a reflection of Holy Love. The rosary is the anchor of the Remnant Faithful amidst a sea of lies and confusion. Entrust the faith of your hearts to Me, the Protectress of your faith, and do not be misled by those who do not know Me.

Dear children, every rosary you pray from the heart is Heaven's weapon of mass destruction against evil. The evils of the day demand your attentive prayers, your aggressive prayers. Do not allow Satan to discourage you by way of hopelessness.

The world without your prayers would be the definition of hopelessness. Evil would prevail in every heart. These days there are whole areas of the world where this is so. The news is filled with every sort of evil plot and action on the part of individuals and certain groups. These cannot be explained away in any manner except to acknowledge Satan's influence over hearts. These events must encourage your prayers, not discourage them.

Dear children, God has given you some good leaders, but their voices have been overpowered by the din of liberals. Many who are now in leadership roles are only politically motivated and do not lead towards the welfare of the world. This generation has been given the gift—the weapon—of the Rosary of the Unborn. Use it to defeat the evil that politics has put in place. It is your lifeline between free will and God's Divine Will. Do not allow the issue of the sale of body parts from unborn children to quiet down. This is a glimpse into the reality of the evil of abortion."

Through the prayers of the rosary every evil that threatens life as you know it can be defeated. The rosary can expose the evil that is in hearts before it spills out into the world. A devotion to the holy rosary is a special sign of predestination.

Dear little children, you do not realize the threat of evil all around you. You do not realize how much I need your prayers. Please join Me in the destruction of Satan's plans which begin by presenting good as evil and evil as good, and end in the condemnation of every soul. Devote the rest of your lives to Satan's defeat by praying the rosary.

∽

Dear reader, please take a few minutes to allow the power of what you have just read in these supernatural messages sink into your hearts. These are words allegedly from Heaven—from Jesus, Mary, and Saint Joseph. Only the individual reading these messages can truly discern their grace. That discernment can only come from the power of the Holy Spirit. If you wish to read more of the messages, go to the web site of Holy Love.

There is an adage that states: "For those who believe, there is no need for explanation; for those who do not believe, no explanation will suffice!"

Next, we explore the endorsements of several highly respected individuals who have publicly expressed their belief and support for Holy Love Ministries. It is, if you will, simply "icing on the cake!"

NINE

POWERFUL ENDORSEMENTS

As stated earlier in the witness stories, there is no better testimonial of a claimed apparition or locution site, or the alleged seer or receiver of locutions, than by personal witness garnered from its good fruits. Even greater witness is the *validation* from people of accepted stature and noted qualifications in the field of supernatural phenomena. They are more than creditable to give such endorsement.

The list of religious luminaries willing to give public testimony as to the good fruits of Holy Love Ministries is impressive. It includes top qualified theologians, well-known experts and highly recognized and involved lay people. It would be impractical to list all of them due to limited space. The selection is narrowed to what may be considered the very best, who have actually been to Holy Love, met with Maureen and carefully scrutinized the messages.

Before the witness of the theologians, there is an important layperson I wish to include as a witness who has been profoundly touched by Holy Love Ministries. Her name is **Immaculee Ilibagiza**, a refugee and victim of the horrible genocide that occurred in the African country of Rwanda in 1994. The genocide was a well-coordinated attack by the majority Hutu tribe against the minority Tutsi tribe, to which Immaculee belonged.

Today, Immaculee is an internationally acclaimed author and motivational speaker. Her first book, *"Left to Tell: Discovering God Amidst the Rwandan Holocaust"* (2006), is an autobiographical work detailing how she survived during the murderous genocide that took the lives of one million members of the Tutsi tribe. She survived hidden away in a small bathroom no larger than three feet long and four feet wide, for 91 days with seven other women. The bathroom was concealed in a room behind a wardrobe in the home of a Hutu Protestant pastor who had been friends with her family for many years.

Hutu civilians and soldiers killed almost all of Immaculee's family members: her mother, her father, and her two brothers Damascene and Vianney. The only other survivor in her family was her brother Aimable, who was studying out of the country in Senegal during the time of the genocide.

In her book *"Left to Tell"*, Immaculee shares how her Roman Catholic faith guided her through her terrible ordeal, especially by praying the rosary. However, the power of her story revolves around the act of her later literally seeking out those who killed her family and telling them in person that she has forgiven them. Such an act is incomprehensible in today's world.

Immaculee was later fortunate to secure a job with the United Nations, which eventually brought her to the United States. Her first concern was to find a place similar to the famous Kibeho apparition site in her native land, which had deeply touched her and changed her life. Kibeho is a small village where the Blessed Virgin Mary began appearing to several teenage girls enrolled in the school located there. The apparitions began on November 28, 1981, the same year as the Medjugorje apparitions began.

Immaculee searched for a long time before coming across a short commentary on Holy Love Ministries in Elyria, Ohio. She felt something inside her confirming this was the place she was seeking and immediately made plans to visit the site as soon as possible.

Several days later, Immaculee took a bus to Cleveland, Ohio, a trip that should have taken only five hours. However, the bus broke down and it was near midnight when it arrived in the city. By the time Immaculee was able to find the property it was closed. Not to be deterred, she wandered around the grounds of Holy Love for hours on her own. She was immediately convinced that this was a holy place very much like Kibeho—the place she had been looking for.

Immaculee was able to return to Holy Love on a weekend several months later. It was while on the grounds of the Ministry on this second trip that she received a cell phone call that her first book had been accepted for publication by a national publishing house, an event that she knew was not just a coincidence. Since the early visits, Immaculee has been on pilgrimage to Holy Love many times. In the spring of 2015, she was invited to give her testimony at Holy Love before an overflowing crowd. By the end of the event, there was no doubt in the hearts of those in attendance that Immaculee Ilibagiza strongly believed in the messages of Holy Love Ministries.

~

The testimony of the theological scholars included in this chapter, goes a long way to giving comfort to all of the people involved with the Ministry. It also supplies good "food for thought" to the skeptics and doubters—not to mention positive theological support.

We begin with the **Rev. Father Albert J. Herbert, S.M.,** a renowned Catholic priest and author of 17 books in the twentieth and twenty-first centuries. However, Fr. Hebert is mostly known as a highly respected expert and reputed author on modern day apparitions and visionaries. He has authored four supernatural-oriented books; yet, he is best known for his book titled: "The Three Days of Darkness," a prophesized event connected to most major present day claimed apparitions.

Father Hebert also wrote the forward to a Holy Love Ministries book titled " Heaven's Last Call." He had this to say about Maureen and Holy Love in the forward, after his own investigation and abundant time spent with visionary Maureen:

"Every wise person seeks to grow in virtue and with the grace of God to work toward spiritual perfection. Ordinary and convenient means for this growth abound in the daily teachings of the Church, through the Mass and the sacraments, and by the good example of others, especially holy persons and the saints. Indeed, if anyone consistently tried to live simply by the two Great Commandments, love of God and neighbor, one could easily become a saint.

"A merciful and generous God gives us extra help. One way is through what is called "private revelation." This term is not the happiest one, because many such revelations are aimed by God at the entire Catholic Church and the whole world. Some examples are Lourdes, Fatima, and the Divine Mercy of God revelations through Sr. Faustina Kowalska [Now a saint]. Some revelations involve extensive instructions and messages, such as the ongoing ones at Medjugorje and some other places.

"The primary focus should be *on the messages and not the messenger* [emphasis added]. What is important is to read the messages, act on them, and see if the results "bear good fruit." Are they worthwhile, helpful, leading one to a holier life? This is especially important in these times when faith and morals are being attacked on all sides and in insidious or even brutal ways.

"The contributor of this Foreword draws on long experience with many visionaries, and also has known this particular messenger [Maureen] for some years. He believes, in his own personal and private opinion, that *these messages constitute an authentic private revelation* [emphasis added]. But again, the important thing is to read the messages, grasp the truth of their teachings, and observe one's own reactions.

"If a person stranded ashore on some deserted island came across a map sticking out of the sand, and found that the map pointed to a hidden treasure, that person would scarcely just look at the map, throw it away, or pay no attention to the instructions. Most people would immediately read and follow the instructions and so find the treasure.

"If a very important document arrived via fax machine or was typed on a typewriter, no one would just stand in admiration of the fax machine or want to go contemplate the typewriter on which the message was written - they grasp the message and act on it!

"So be it with these messages, perhaps better called 'teachings'. They are perfectly in accord with Catholic faith and morals, and indeed, with living a high spiritual life. Other priests have also evaluated them as good."

—Albert J. Hebert, S.M.

Father Hebert's testimony could actually stand alone as strong verification of Holy Love given his expertise in the field. It is powerful, confirming and straightforward. Here is a good priest of the Roman Catholic Church who devoted his life to the study of apparitions and other religious phenomena. He is revered at Holy Love for not wavering in the face of opposition to the Ministry from the Cleveland Diocese. He came; he observed; and, he believed.

~

We continue with further confirming testimony from the late Reverend **Dr. Gabriel Ganaka, O.F.R.,** who was the Archbishop of Jos in Nigeria, Africa. He rose rapidly in the ranks of holy service to the Church to eventually being appointed archbishop by Pope Paul VI in 1975.

The challenges continued to come over the years of service and the Archbishop proved equal to the tasks of each advancement step in his career. Hence, he made a huge success of it when he was appointed by Pope Paul VI as a member of the Canon Law Review Commission and the Pontifical Council for inter-religious Dialogue.

Archbishop Ganaka was able to travel extensively throughout the world; he spoke several languages including fluent English. In December 1995, the Archbishop took ill and was flown to the United States for treatment. He collapsed and died suddenly in November 1999.

Prior to his death, the Archbishop spent much time at Holy Love and, as with Father Hebert, was able to be with Maureen for extended periods of time.

Here are excerpts that the Archbishop wrote from the forward of a volume of messages given to Maureen at Holy Love:

"The messages contained here cover a wide range of subjects, which should provide the interested reader with very many themes for reflection, meditation for Christian living aimed at growth in holiness. Subjects covered, to name a few, include abortion, angels, Co-Redemptrix, Mediatrix and Advocate. Others are Divine Love, Divine Mercy, the Eucharist, holiness, prayer and sacrifice. Various teachings on the priesthood and many key virtues such as humility, surrender, meekness, trust, patience, forgiveness, obedience, faith, hope and compassion are also included. It is a book that should not be read at one setting; it is one that should be prayerfully read and meditated upon for one's spiritual growth section by section... It is true that the events happening in Elyria, Ohio have not been investigated by the [Catholic] Church as yet; the messages, however, are so simple yet deep and profound. The rate at which the messages are being received, at times thrice a day, yet rich in variety and profundity, *could not possibly be the invention of a mere mortal* [emphasis added]. Without preempting any eventual final verdict there may be in the future, suffice it to say here that our arch-enemy Satan could not possibly call ceaselessly for love of God and of neighbor, for prayer and sacrifice, for holiness of life, the frequent and worthy reception of the sacraments, and for the use of the sacramentals.

…The messages concerning the United Hearts of Jesus and Mary are rich as they are varied. These must be studied. Heaven has given mighty promises for use of the devotional chaplet and scapular of the United Heart requested. The Confraternity of the United Hearts that is soon to be initiated will exist, among other things, to propagate understanding of this revelation, its impact on personal holiness, and devotion to the United Hearts through this chaplet and scapular."

Archbishop Ganaka's words are powerful confirmation of the many messages Maureen receives at Holy Love. His testimony, along with that of Father Hebert stands in stark contrast to the negative efforts of the bishop of the Cleveland Diocese to stop people from coming to Holy Love.

∼

As we continue, yet another priest adds to the accolades given to Holy Love. He is **Father Edward O'Connor** who upon receiving his doctorate degree in theology in 1952 has taught at the University of Notre Dame ever since and has authored many books focused on Marian apparitions.

I was privileged to be on the grounds at Holy Love several years ago when Fr. O'Connor was also there. We were able to speak at length about Holy Love. It was clear to me that this man's accomplishments as a professor at Notre Dame and as a writer on Marian apparitions were well deserved from his tedious research and adherence to the traditions of the Catholic Church. He was so moved by the messages received by Maureen that he felt called to write a letter to the bishop of the Cleveland Diocese in support of Holy Love. Here are the major excerpts of what he wrote directly to Bishop Lennon in a letter dated July 28, 2008:

"I would like to testify that I have known Mrs. Kyle for about 15 years, have heard her speak, and have read her messages carefully. It is my opinion that these messages are authentic; furthermore, that the spiritual counsel they offer is not only sound but also remarkably profound.

"I realize that some people, members of the clergy included, are very hostile to her work; but this has been the case with Lourdes, Fatima, and just about every other Marian apparition. When it becomes appropriate for the diocese to take a stance in regard to Mrs. Kyle, I suggest that first, a commission of impartial theologians be appointed to study her messages and evaluate them from a doctrinal point of view. If they do not contain any errors, then the diocese could very well wait and see the fruits of Mrs. Kyle's work. "By their fruits you will know them" is the criterion Jesus gave for judging those who claim to prophesy in His name. I expect that you will find her a real blessing for your diocese."

Of course, true to form, there was no response from the Cleveland Diocese to Fr. O'Connor's letter.

≈

The list of prominent theologians endorsing Holy Love includes the late **Archbishop Roman Danylak,** of Toronto, Canada. Let it suffice to say that he was well qualified to professionally endorse the visionary and the messages of Holy Love. He was also a personal friend to me and we spent much time together discussing the apparitions of Medjugorje. Here is what Archbishop Danylak wrote in a letter of approbation:

"What reason could there be to involve the Angelic Doctor in the issues of Holy Love, if it be true, as the supporters of this Mission and Maureen Sweeney-Kyle claim?

"As I carefully perused the sixty-some pages of the messages or responses given by St. Thomas Aquinas, to the Mission of Holy Love, the Divine Will and the Chambers of the United Hearts of Holy Love and Divine Love, I was overwhelmed by the simplicity and profundity of the answers that St. Thomas gave in his pithy responses over a period of six years, as he expounded in masterly fashion the profound truths of our faith. They surpass the capacities of Maureen and the group of people working with her, and of most theologians. They manifest the profound insights of the author of the Summa Theologiae.

"But the question still remains, why would the Divine Master and Teacher, why would the Queen of Heaven, relegate to this Doctor of the Faith, the task of expounding these fundamentals of sublime truths? And the answer is threefold. Heaven so willed it. Willed to choose to send this master theologian, whom the Church acknowledges as the common Doctor of Faith and Doctrine.

"In another context, as I read the message that our Lord Jesus had given another visionary - Julia Kim - Jesus identifies the spirit of rationalism as the original sin of our age, a rationalism that dominates the minds of many ecclesiastics who find it difficult, if not impossible, to believe with simple faith the truths of Heaven. Nor is this the fault of our own century and of the Church of today, it wasn't only Thomas the Apostle who needed to place his finger in the wounds of Christ's hands and his fist into the wound of His Heart. All the Apostles but two had taken off in this hour of darkness when Satan dominated and Christ hung on the cross, abandoning their Master, their friend, their God. When Jesus appeared to the eleven, the evening of the Sunday of Resurrection, it took them some time to accept the reality that Jesus was risen and was standing among them in His resurrected and glorious body.

"The third reason is the fact that even the spiritual directors who have been involved with Maureen Sweeney-Kyle and her messages, and the theologians who have come to know these messages of the Divine Will of the Divine and Holy Love, of the Love of the Immaculate Mother of God and the Mysteries of the Chambers of the Heart of Jesus, find it difficult to express and explain in simpler language the truth and extent of these messages. It was only as I read and perused these pages of the messages given to Maureen by St. Thomas Aquinas that I began to understand and to believe the profound doctrine contained in them.

I present these thoughts in lieu of a nihil obstat and imprimatur to this booklet of the messages of St. Thomas Aquinas and commend them to especially the ecclesiastics, that is, the clergy of today that they might grow in love and in trust of divine goodness."

∾

Lastly, just to put a little glitter on this extremely relevant chapter, we add one more strong endorsement—again by a Roman Catholic priest, who also served as Maureen's spiritual director for several years:

"It would seem reasonable that if you are permitted to speak and write about private revelations, you should also be permitted to investigate them and visit the places where they take place. If nobody ever went to such places, there would be no reason for bishops or Rome to take any action. It would also seem proper for bishops to remain neutral regarding reported private revelations until and unless they conduct a proper investigation. *A non-approval is not a disapproval* (emphasis in italics added). Usually, waiting for an official Church approval would take several lifetimes.

"Maureen Sweeney-Kyle's private revelations have been accompanied by claims of healings, conversions, miraculous signs in the heavens, instant changes of rosary chains to a gold color, and other supernatural phenomena. The fundamental message of Holy Love is at the heart and center of the teachings of Christ and His Church. Loving God and loving our neighbor sums up all His teaching. Maureen has been called to spread that message all over America and beyond. She has spoken to thousands of people in over a dozen states of America and also in Ireland. Many thousands of people have come to pray and listen to her messages at the ministry's headquarters in Elyria, Ohio.

"For me to be asked to be her spiritual director has been a great blessing. Besides spiritual graces, I have been healed of a heart palpitation condition. The quality and frequency of her messages from both Jesus and Mary is extraordinary. While Mary has stopped visiting on a regular basis to many other reported visionaries, at this writing both Jesus and Mary still continue regular visits to Maureen.

"Faithful and devoted lay people are the backbone for the support of private revelations and their propagation. Authentic private revelations promote faith, prayer in general, and above all, attending Mass, receiving the Sacraments and living the Christian life to the full. The ministry of Holy Love, as I see it, has no other purpose."

Reverend Frank Kenney S.M., ST.D. - Doctor of Marian Theology, Catholic University of America (Given on January 1, 1998).

Once again, what more needs to be added to such profound witness and important endorsements? The very fact that these Catholic priests, all of them so well-qualified, would give endorsement to Holy Love Ministries, stands in stark contrast to the opposition of the bishop(s) of the Cleveland Diocese.

~

Message given to Maureen on March 4, 2015:

Dear children, you know from experience that if you venture outside in bitter cold weather and any part of you is left unprotected such as fingers or your nose, you run the risk of frostbite. The spiritual climate in the world today is like the bitter cold. You must cover yourself with prayer. If you have any fear in your heart, ask the angels to surround you and to protect you. If your faith is challenged, ask for My Protection as Mary, Protectress the Faith. I will come immediately to your aid. If you lack trust, ask Me to increase the love in your heart. If you are uncertain as to a course of some action, ask the Holy Spirit for Wisdom. You must never run the risk of going out into the spiritually cold world unprotected, where danger is all around you. The enemy of your salvation sees clearly his every inroad to your wellbeing. When you begin to lose the peace in your heart, understand that this is the first sign of Satan's frostbite. It is then you should cover yourself even more with prayer.

TEN

COME AND SEE

Now you know about the beginning, growth and ongoing spiritual success of Holy Love Ministries. You have read the witness stories of pilgrims who have been there. You have also read the incredible endorsements of recognized theologians, all of which are Catholic priests!

There is nothing more to say other than--come and see for your self!

What better way to answer doubts about Holy Love, Medjugorje or any other claimed apparition site or other supernatural occurrence than to find out personally by visiting the site to see first hand? A common trait for such places as Holy Love is an inundation of unfounded rumor, gossip and outright untruths usually perpetrated by individuals or groups who rather than conducting a proper discernment by visiting and investigating, judge from a distance. Thus, the invitation again to come and see and experience the graces of Holy Love.

The pilgrims who come to Holy Love spend time in and around the different parts of the site. As if giving a spiritual guided tour, Blessed Virgin stated in one message to Maureen: *Please understand, my children, the layout of this property represents the soul's journey into holiness and our United Hearts.*

Each special location is based on prayers and reported spiritual miracles that have occurred at that location. Massive crowds attend special feast day celebrations and wander through the area. Every evening there is the praying of the rosary and on special occasions, speakers are invited to come and give personal witness.

Let's take a quick tour of just what pilgrims find when making pilgrimage to Holy Love:

As you enter the property there is a modest-sized brick sign welcoming visitors to Holy Love Ministries and Shrine with the words: An "Ecumenical Ministry and Shrine."

The sign again establishes the fact that this is a place for all people of all faiths.

A large brick complex named the Saint Thomas Aquinas Learning Center greets visitors a short distance from the entrance. It is a multi-purpose structure with ample facilities that includes a large auditorium primarily used for indoor talks and as a place of prayer. It is complete with a modern commercial kitchen and cafeteria to service pilgrims. There is also a large gift and bookstore filled with information about Holy Love.

The building is also equipped with meeting rooms for retreats or special events. Pilgrims can find information on the shrine here as well. Surrounding it is a massive parking area, usually filled with large buses that come to the Shrine from distant places.

Beyond the Learning Center scattered throughout the sprawling property are a variety of small structures, lakes and shrines, each a site designated for special prayers. One of the lakes represents Our Lady of Sorrows and is named the Lake of Tears, where pilgrims can purge their souls of the most flagrant faults that prevent complete conversion. From there one can move to the Lake of Angels. Again, this is a special place of prayer and reflection, as well as a moment of acknowledgement of the roles of angels.

The walls of the mini structures near the different places honoring God The Father, Jesus, the Blessed Virgin Mary and several saints and angels are covered with letters of witness from pilgrims attesting to miraculous spiritual and physical healings credited to Holy Love through these extraordinary sites on the property.

The largest shrine area is that of The United Hearts Field, where the apparitions take place in front of massive crowds on feast days throughout the year. Again, it is a special place of grace, prayer and reflection on the spiritual life. Just being present for an apparition at this holy place is a grace, most especially when one is surrounded by thousands of pilgrims filled with happiness and peace.

Arguably the most popular spot on the property is Maranatha Spring, where pilgrims can bless themselves and fill containers with the holy waters of the spring. This incredible gift of grace is the source of literally thousands of physical and spiritual healings. Upon its location when the second and present property was purchased as the permanent home of Holy Love Ministries, the Blessed Virgin said: *Joyfully, I reveal to you today that the waters of Maranatha are as the Lourdes of this continent. They are comparable in healing grace, both in body and soul. They are much like the cascade in Betania. Therefore, you can propagate it with much faith and hope.* (May 31, 1995)

Here are two other messages the Blessed Mother has given concerning the Spring:

(1) *The hour of my predilection is at hand and will be shown through God's will and grace at the site of Maranatha Spring—all for the greater honor and glory of the most Blessed Trinity. I am opening my heart to all nations at this sight and through the favor of my grace, reconciling the lost to God.* (February 9, 1996)

(2) *I am continually present and awaiting all mankind at Maranatha Spring. It is here I will comfort and console those who come to me. I desire as my Son allows, to alleviate afflictions and render certain and untold grace. Ask my children to surrender their petitions to me at the Spring.* (August 8, 1996)

Lastly, on August 2, 2009 the Blessed Virgin gave this important message:

On the property here, the angel that is assigned each soul at Maranatha Spring tries to bring the peace of Holy Love into the soul he is assigned. The angel tries to inspire the message of Holy Love to come alive in the heart of the soul, no matter his faith, creed or lack thereof.

It is recommended that pilgrims say this prayer whenever any water from the Spring is used in making the sign of the cross:

Dear Jesus, as I bless myself with this water, open my heart to the grace Heaven desires I have. Let me look into my soul with the eyes of truth. Give me the courage and humility to do so. Heal me according to the will of your Father. Amen.

Thus, as stated so often in the preceding chapters, Holy Love offers visiting pilgrims a place to spend time in prayer and meditation. It leads one to wonder why anyone would oppose such a place of prayer and healing.

Despite the opposition and disbelief of some skeptics, Holy Love Ministries continues to draw thousands to its grounds. People are hungry for solutions to personal problems and many come out of curiosity to see if they might receive answers. What they usually find is that the answers come through prayer and witness.

∾

To put it plain and simple, come and see for yourself what Holy Love Ministries is about. Come, as I did, along with literally tens of thousands of pilgrims over its thirty years of existence. I am sure you will find the same spiritual gifts awaiting you!

The grace, peace and love of our Lord Jesus Christ be with you always.